Time and Worldmaking

Time and Worldmaking

John Frame and the Reformational Philosophies

Tim Wilder

Via Moderna Books
2024

ISBN 979-8-9883645-8-0

Font: Aldine 401 (Bitstream); Titles: Bembo Std
System: Affinity Publisher

Cover art: Left panel, The Garden of Earthly Delights (detail)
    Hieronymus Bosch, between 1480 and 1510

Via Moderna Books, Rapid City
2024

CONTENTS

Preface	1
John Frame's Critique Of The Amsterdam Philosophy	5
Character of the Reformational Philosophy	8
A Metaphysical View	8
Differences Between Dooyeweerd and Vollenhoven	10
Frame's Explanation of Reformational Philosophy	12
Van Til's View of Revelation and Language	23
Other Writings By John Frame	33
The Word of God in the Cosmonomic Philosophy	33
What is God's Word?	35
Reply to Prof. Zylstra	35
Toronto, Reformed Orthodoxy, and the Word of God: Where Do We Go from Here?	38
Report by Cory Gress On Reformational Philosophy	41
Reply by Aldolfo García De La Sienra	49
Evaluation	61
Van Til's Interpretation of Reformational Philosophies	62
Van Til's Break From Dooyeweerd	68
Who Was the Problem in 1972?	71
The Canadians Again	72
The Big Picture	73
Citations And Further Reading	77
Index	79

PREFACE

This little book is a review and discussion of a series of booklets that primarily involve John Frame's analysis and criticism of the Reformational Philosophies, which he called at the time the Amsterdam Philosophy. The debate had a practical origin.

John Frame published his critique of the Reformational Philosophy in 1972. He called it "Preliminary" and it was a response to problems being experienced by people who were seeking to respond to the rise of anti-Christian secularism by founding Christian institutions, such as schools. They found that they were opposed within their own circles by a group that insisted that such alternatives to the state institutions ought not to be Christian either. Frame reports their position as that "the church is a faith institution, while the school is an analytic institution. The two belong to different modal spheres, and thus can never share a common basis." This is not the usual objection to anything "Christian" outside of "spiritual" matters that comes so frequently, and even more in those days, from the advocates of pietistic withdrawal. There was a peculiar and seemingly incomprehensible theory behind it.

After enjoying some initial circulation as a booklet, the essay lay dormant for a time, though now it is easily available as a PDF download from the well-known Frame-Poythress website about their Triperspectival Theology. Recently, a translation into Spanish was published in Mexico and a response appeared, in both English and Spanish, from the Cántaro Institute in Canada. Apparently, they are Baptists. (They cite the 1689 Baptist Confession as expressing their convictions.) They appear to be that rarity, right-wing Dooyeweerdians. Both groups also promote the works of Cornelius Van Til.

A problem with this particular debate is that, as John Frame notes in a preface added in 2005, he has been charged with not knowing Dooyeweerd. The book has not been updated or otherwise added to by Frame. Having drawn his observations from works of the Reformational philosophers, Frame seems confident of his account of them. Its problem, however, is a failure to distinguish the different Reformational philosophies. His main notions are taken from Dooyeweerd's popular lecture series, *In the Twilight of Western Thought*, mixed with references to J. M. Spier's *An Introduction to Christian Philosophy*. This failure to distinguish the philosophies is possible because he omits a proper account of the very different metaphysical models of Herman Dooyeweerd and Dirk Vollenhoven. That they differed much seems to be unknown to Frame and he also resists understanding these philosophies on the basis of what their metaphysics requires the systems to be. Writing in 2011, Frame still presents Dooyeweerd and Vollenhoven as having a unified philosophy, based on the analysis of the modal spheres and seeking "to apply [Abraham] Kuyper's vision to philosophy."[1]

A second problem is that Frame only hesitantly acknowledges the thirty-five-year period of endorsement of the Reformational philosophies by Cornelius Van Til, their influence on Van Til's apologetics, for which Frame has become the spokesman, and the degree to which this was incorporated into the theological training at Westminster Seminary. Frame, in 2011, mentions that no one on the [Westminster] faculty wanted to offend Van Til who was "deeply committed to Kuyper's vision."[2] The Reformational Philosophy, however, is rather more than Kuyper's vision. Further, Van Til's agenda seems to have been the replacement of the Presbyterian theological tradition with the neo-Calvinist one, though he made a formal reference to the Princeton Seminary tradition.

Frame also mentions, in 2011, the further development out of Westminster roots of Christian Reconstruction, which he equates with theonomy. In fact, Christian Reconstruction, through Rousas Rushdoony, was a promoter and publisher of works of the Dooyeweerdian school and other CR writers, such as James Jordan, were early saturated with it. They saw it as essentially compatible with the thought of Van Til, with which they also identified.[3] Fused with its apparent opposite (yet showing Dooyeweerdian characteristics, as

---

[1] John Frame, *The Escondido Theology* (Lakeland, Florida: Whitefield Media Productions, 2011), p. 6.

[2] Frame, *Escondido Theology*, p. 10.

[3] Both the Chalcedon and Tyler versions saw themselves as furthering Van Til's heritage. See Gary North, *Westminster's Confession: The Abandonment*

will appear below), that is, Meredith Kline's symbolic theology, this also became an inspiration for the ecclesiocentric Federal Vision theology.[4]

Much more broadly, the Reformational Philosophies have had an influence on worldview apologetics in general, principally through Francis Schaeffer, and the adoption of this approach by InterVarsity Press in the 1970s. Schaeffer was a student of Van Til but was also directly in touch with Dutch thinkers. The influence is evident in his popularization of the Ground-motive approach to analyzing intellectual history.

The issues raised by Frame's critique continue to be important.

There are further questions, however, about how this situation came about – that these philosophical systems came to be admitted to the foundations of the theology being used to train the ministers of Presbyterian denominations and of the literature of influential movements of Christian thought. They were accepted and taught as the only sound response to the hostile modern ideologies. A parallel set of questions could also be asked of the various Dutch Reformed denominations and schools, for example, Calvin College. A different set of answers would be given. There was, however, a different status to Reformational Philosophies in those places, leaving aside the special institutions created to propagate it, such as the Toronto Institute of Christian Studies.

Frame writes, that "It used to be that a Professor of Apologetics at Westminster had to be committed to Van Til's apologetic method." This became mandatory even though Van Til "took exception to most all of the church's past thinking on epistemology and apologetics." We can still see this attitude in Westminster, Philadelphia where a wall of protection has been erected around the current Van Til spokesman, K. Scott Oliphint. But in Westminster, California there "was a stunning reversal: from the dominant Van Tillian Kuyperianism of Westminster/Philadelphia, to a repudiation of this view as heresy."[5] On the Dutch side, while raw Reformationalism was pro-

---

of Van Til's Legacy (Tyler, Texas: Institute for Christian Economics, 1991) for his interpretation.

[4] Klien's *Images of the Spirit* (Wipf and Stock, reprint, 1999) was particularly influential on the Tyler branch of Christian Reconstruction.

[5] Frame, *Escondido Theology*, pp. 12, 13.

moted much more vigorously and clearly than at Westminster, there were, at Calvin College for example, always alternative views, with the best-known faculty being of a different persuasion.

There were "partisan battles" at Westminster, Philadelphia about Dooyeweerd's influence, as Frame relates, but somehow it did not seem to touch areas where the philosophy was incorporated in a softer form, as in Van Til's apologetics. At least Frame does not report it, nor does he think this is something to be remarked upon. Yet the impression is that the problems Frame sought to address in his booklet were brought about to a significant degree by the complicity of his own seminary in the spread of these philosophies.

Out of Westminister, California has come a book by J. V. Fesko, *Reforming Apologetics: Retrieving the Classic Reformed Approach to Defending the Faith*.[6] The book is not very good; Fesko seems to be writing outside of his field. But its point is clear. He is retrieving an approach that Van Til discarded. But it is not the Princeton tradition, but scholasticism that he primarily has in mind. This makes clear that the debate has changed since 1972. It is no longer a question of rejecting the particular approach of the Reformational modal theories, as something that can be distinguished from Van Til's thought, but of discarding something that is labeled the Kuyperian vision. I have two points to make about this. First, Van Til's thought cannot be wholly separated from the Reformational Philosophy. Second, though this is largely argued elsewhere,[7] even the Westminister, California (Escondido) theology bears the imprint of Kuyperianism.

---

[6] J. V. Fesko, *Reforming Apologetics: Retrieving the Classic Reformed Approach to Defending the Faith* (Grand Rapids: Baker Academic, 2019). Formerly at Westminster, Fesko now teaches at Reformed Theological Seminary.

[7] Tim Wilder, *Theosophy, Van Til, and Bahnsen: How Neo-Calvinism Deformed Apologetics* (Rapid City: Via Moderna Books, 2023).

JOHN FRAME'S CRITIQUE OF THE AMSTERDAM PHILOSOPHY

In 1972 John Frame published a criticism of what he called the Amsterdam Philosophy.[8] He spoke of the philosophy being at that time about fifty years old. In his opening paragraph he describes the wide extent of the movement's influence, with its own institutions as well as committed members employed as professors at various colleges and universities. It was, then, very late for an establishment voice in the Presbyterian world to initiate a criticism.

In a Preface added in 2005 Frame says the booklet was published by Pilgrim Press. There is a version by Harmony Press, also dated 1972, that binds Frame's work with an essay by Leonard J. Coppes. Frame's work was translated into Spanish and published by Reforma Press in Mexico, in an undated publication, this time in combination with an essay, "A Report from the Desert" by a Protestant Reformed pastor, Cory Gress. Finally, a response to Frame from the Amsterdam side appeared from Cántaro Publications, in February 2024, written by Adolfo García de la Sienra Guajardo. The elephant in the room, however, is still J. Glenn Friesen's *Neo-Calvinism and Christian Theosophy: Franz von Baader, Abraham Kuyper, Herman Dooyeweerd*.[9] While completely friendly to Herman Dooyeweerd's version of the Amsterdam Philosophy, it is also devastating in his demonstration that it is a speculative theosophy, arising from roots in nineteenth-century theosophical writers.

At the time of Frame's writing, however, a critical study of the movement's origins, as provided by Friesen, was not available. What

---

[8] The PDF version of Frame's essay is available online, but without page numbers. https://frame-poythress.org/wp-content/uploads/2012/08/FrameJohnAmsterdamPhilosophy1972.pdf

[9] J. Glenn Friesen, *Neo-Calvinism and Christian Theosophy: Franz von Baader, Abraham Kuyper, Herman Dooyeweerd* (Calgary: Aevum Books, 2015, 2016, 2021)

was known were the writings of various advocates of the movement and a recognition that its prime builders were Herman Dooyeweerd and Dirk Vollenhoven of the Free University of Amsterdam and H. G. Stoker of South Africa. Most significant was a long-standing relationship with Westminster Seminary, which Frame mentions, but he does not go into his role as the new voice for just that Kuyperian element in Westminster Seminary.

While Frame refers to this movement as the "Amsterdam Philosophy", preferring this to such alternatives as "The Philosophy of the Idea of Law", "The Philosophy of the Cosmonomic Idea", or simply "Dooyeweerdianism", it is the name "Reformational Philosophy" that seems to have caught on more largely internationally. Frame objects to this name as "too honorific for use in a context of debate." It is, however, under the label "Reformational" that people are more likely to encounter the movement, and as long as this is distinguished from "Reformed", this is the name that will probably provide the most clarity of reference.

Frame says, "In North America, for many years, the leading proponent of this movement was generally acknowledged to be Prof. Cornelius Van Til of Westminster Theological Seminary, Philadelphia." He footnotes this with "Dr. Van Til is still listed as an editor of *Philosophia Reformata*, and the 1968 printing of Dooyeweerd's *In the Twilight of Western Thought* (Nutley, Craig Press, 1960) lists him as a member of the school (p. 197). As we shall see, however, Dr. Van Til has become increasingly critical of the movement in recent years; so critical, in fact, that it would be inaccurate to regard him now as a member of this school." Frame goes on to note that Van Til's "influence was perhaps the major factor in attracting such younger men as H. Evan Runner (now of Calvin College) and Robert D. Knudsen (now of Westminster Seminary) into the Amsterdam circle."

It was in 1936 that Van Til began his formal association with the movement, accepting an editorship for *Philosophia Reformata*. There is some limited comment on this in the scholarly literature. Timothy L. McConnel notes that Van Til's only publication in the journal was an article in 1937 and suggests that "his co-editorship was a token position, to add an American name to an otherwise Dutch journal."[10]

---

[10] Timothy L. McConnell, "The Influence of Idealism on the Apologetics of Cornelius Van Til", *JETS* 48-3 (September 2005) p. 573, n61.

Laurence R. O'Donnell reports that "the scholarly relationship between ... Cornelius Van Til ... and Dutch Reformed philosopher, Herman Dooyeweerd (1894-1977) remains largely unexplored in the secondary literature attending both thinkers. The scant extant scholarship on this topic consists mostly of passing remarks regarding alleged disagreements between the two thinkers."[11]

At Westminster Seminary, where Frame taught, however, the connection was not of trivial consequence. There was an acrimonious controversy among the Westminster faculty over differences including the Reformational philosophy, with personal verbal attacks by faculty on each other. An account of this by Ian Hewitson is in his *Trust and Obey* (with a Forward by John Frame).[12] His thesis is that Norman Shepherd was caught up in the bitterness that accompanied this controversy. As a partisan of Shepherd's, he omits Shepherd's role in the controversy including his attacks on Dooyeweerd and Robert Knudsen from the classroom lectern.

After Frame began to teach at Westminster, he was asked by Van Til to teach some apologetics classes. In that field, he became more a professor of Van Tillianism than of apologetics. He also came into conflict with the Dooyeweerd faction. As Frame describes it:

> When I arrived, many students at Westminster were disciples of the Dutch Calvinistic philosopher Herman Dooyeweerd. These students tended to be pretty arrogant, arguing that the traditional Reformed theology that Westminster represented was "dualist," "scholastic," and so on. Eventually I found myself at odds with them and their ideology. I was particularly concerned about their doctrine of revelation, in which the authority of Scripture was limited to the "realm of faith" and our main guidance for life was to be found, not in Scripture at all, but rather in the "word of creation," i.e., natural revelation understood through the lens of Dooyeweerd's philosophy.[13]

---

[11] Laurence R. O'Donnell, *An Analysis of Cornelius Van Til's Presupposition of Reformed Dogmatics with special reference to Herman Bavinck's Geremormeede Dogmatiek* (Master's thesis, Calvin Theological Seminary, 2011), p. 172.

[12] Ian A. Hewitson, *Trust and Obey: Norman Shepherd & the Justification Controversy at Westminster Theological Seminary* (Apple Valley, Minn.: NextStep Resources, 2011).

[13] John M. Frame, "Backgrounds to My Thought", https://framepoythress.org/about/john-frame-full-bio/

What Frame calls the "arrogance" of the students is that they held what Dooyeweerd (and their teachers) taught as a major point. If one is going to allow Dooyeweerdianism, and even teach it in the seminary, then why balk at the consequence that some students actually will hold it? But what this gets into is that there is an aspect of Van Til's thought that goes along with Dooyeweerd on some of this and an aspect that goes against it, and it is Van Til who was inconsistent. This will become clearer when Frame explains some of Van Til's objections to Dooyeweerd below.

Character of the Reformational Philosophy

Having outlined the extent of the growth and influence of the Reformational Philosophy, Frame warns that "not *all* of the comments made about the movement in the following pages will apply to *all* of its adherents." As it is succinct I will quote Frame's own summary of his criticism.

> The trouble is, however, that these scriptural, Reformational, brilliantly well-expressed principles are not "all there is" in the Amsterdam philosophy. Unfortunately, these emphases are mixed in with others, which in our view are not scriptural, not Reformational, and not particularly clearly expressed, either. That is to say: (1) The writings of this movement are full of unclear statements, invalid arguments, and general intellectual shoddiness. This criticism is not as serious as (2) below, but it is a serious one. Such lack of rigor in a Christian philosophy is not pleasing to God. It will not do for Christians to support a second-rate philosophical system simply because that system claims to be Christian or even because it is Christian in some respects. But further (2) The writings of this movement contain a substantial amount of demonstrably unscriptural, and therefore false, teaching. These two criticisms will be documented in what follows.

What is remarkable about (1) is that it so directly applies to the Van Til movement, in which John Frame spent his professional life.

A Metaphysical View

Before entering into the detail of Frame's discussion of the Reformation philosophy, a brief explanation in outline of it is necessary. It will be described from a metaphysical point of view, in the manner that Friesen mainly analyses it in his book. Frame will approach it from the perspective of experience, which will make little sense absent an understanding of how and where that experience takes place in the order of things. In addition, it will quickly appear that we are looking at two different philosophies.

First a few observations about the background to the creation of these philosophies. Dooyeweerd was heavily indebted to 19th century theosophy for his ideas, and his own thought was an amalgamation of theosophy and Kantian idealism. The theosophy of previous eras, for example, that of the most famous theosophist of all, Jacob Boehm, was an esoteric reflection on the cosmos which, studied in the right way, was thought to reveal deep truths about God. A turning point in theosophy was the influence of Kantian idealism on speculative thought in the nineteenth century. From then on it was the reflection on consciousness and the nature of experience that became more important. It was this type of theosophy that influenced theology, including neo-Calvinism, and became a component of Dooyeweerd's thinking along with his direct use of Kant.

Dooyeweerd took over from theosophy an idea about time. Besides the eternal, there is temporal creation. Experience in time is divided between the supratemporal, which Dooyeweerd also called the religious (also it is the "created heaven"), which is the location of the self and the origin of the experience that appears in the temporal. Besides the supratemporal, there is temporal, or cosmic, experience where the unitary experience of the supratemporal emerges and is divided into modalities as light passing through a prism is divided into colors. The modalities in temporal experience are the result of law structures that give a sphere sovereignty to each modality. The law-structures are not the consequence of time, because they have their origin in the supratemporal "nuclear moment" of each modality. The modalities, however, appear in time, and they emerge from an initial naïve experience in a way that philosophy can attend to. Philosophy, using rational thought which is one of the modalities, begins from reflection on experience as it emerges into the temporal and takes on the modal qualities. In the temporal, there are individuality structures, which are the "things" in experience. A test of a philosophy, Dooyeweerd said, was that it must account for the modalities, but also for the initial unitary naïve experience. Because of this focus on the analysis of experience, Dooyeweerd is sometimes classified as a phenomenologist.

Differences Between Dooyeweerd and Vollenhoven

According to Friesen, Vollenhoven and Dooyeweerd disagreed on almost every major point, whether in ontology, epistemology or theology.[14] He lists twenty-four points of difference. (Actually he skips one.) The major and more comprehensible ones are:

1. *Dualism, Monism, Nondualism*. This was a difficult problem for Vollenhoven, whose thought went through modifications. "There is no indication of any understanding of Dooyeweerd's nondualism."

2. *Being and Meaning*. "For Dooyeweerd, God alone is Being ... even our selfhood is not being, but refers to the true being of God." For Vollenhoven "creation does not refer beyond itself."

3. *Place of Law*. "Vollenhoven wants to maintain a strict separation between God and cosmos to avoid pantheism and yet he also wants to allow for God's immanence in the world. The law is the boundary between God and creation. ... But that is very different from God's active involvement in our lives and our mystical participation in Christ, as both Kuyper and Dooyeweerd emphasized."

5. *Cosmic time*. "Dooyeweerd emphasizes that the idea of cosmic time is the basis of his philosophical theory of reality.... Vollenhoven was not using the idea of time that Dooyeweerd obtained from Baader with the distinctions eternal/supratemporal/temporal."

6. *Supratemporal heart*. "Vollenhoven rejected that line of Kuyper's neo-Calvinism that relies on a supratemporal central unity of man's existence.... Influenced by Janse, Vollenhoven later rejected any idea of the immortality of the soul."

7. *Man as image of God*. Contrary to the "reformational principles of the Free University ... based on 'the human being's being created according to God's image', Vollenhoven did not accept such a metaphysical use of 'image of God'.... Dooyeweerd used 'image of God' in the sense of how we, like God, express or reveal ourselves from a higher sphere to a lower."

9. *Self and ego*. "Vollenhoven does not discuss any such distinction, and rejects even the idea of a selfhood."

11. *Modalities*. "Vollenhoven did not agree that modes are modes of

---

[14] J. Glenn Friesen, *Two Paths of Reformational Philosophy: Early Writings of Vollenhoven and Dooyeweerd*, p. 145. Online. https://www.academia.edu/105254020/Two_Paths_of_Reformational_Philosophy_Early_Writings_of_Vollenhoven_and_Dooyeweerd_by

consciousness. But if that is so, then Vollenhoven and Dooyeweerd are not talking about the same idea." "For Dooyeweerd, the modes are given in an order of time; there is an earlier and a later mode; for Vollenhoven, the order is not one of time, but of ever-greater complexity."

12. *Sphere sovereignty*. "Vollenhoven did not like the term 'sphere sovereignty.' ... In any event, he uses the term in a different way from Dooyeweerd..... For Dooyeweerd, sovereignty operates from out of the center. Thus, the central nuclear moment of the modal sphere is what guarantees its sovereignty. The center is supratemporal, thus in a higher region.... Without the idea of supratemporality and the root-unity, and the distinction between center and periphery, Vollenhoven cannot have this same understanding of sphere sovereignty insofar as it relates to modalities."

14. *Specific modalities*. "Apart from disagreeing as to what modalities are, Vollenhoven and Dooyeweerd disagreed as to the nature of specific modalities like the historical."

16. *Theoretical and pre-theoretical*. "Vollenhoven's view of pre-theoretical experience is also different from Dooyeweerd in that he includes under it the information given in Scripture as well as information we receive from others, even if that information was the result of their theoretical work. Neither of these are included in Dooyeweerd's idea of naïve experience. For one thing, Dooyeweerd did not regard Scripture as a source of information....." "Vollenhoven viewed pre-theoretical in terms of 'common sense.'[15] But that places Vollenhoven in the tradition of Thomas Reid, and not Kuyper's neo-Calvinism."

20. *Use of Scripture for philosophy*. "Dooyeweerd did not use Scripture as a source for his philosophy, although he did sometimes show that his philosophy accorded with Scripture. Dooyeweerd's philosophy begins with experience, and he is critical of a propositional use of Scripture. Dooyeweerd denied that issues concerning the nature of the soul, or of creation, fall and redemption, regeneration, revelation or even incarnation could be settled by exegesis of Scripture." "Vollenhoven does use Scripture as a source for knowing."

[For Dooyeweerd "religious" is supratemporal and revelation,

---

[15] This comment should not be taken to indicate an actual understanding of Reid's epistemology or a similarity to it.

creation, fall, redemption, etc. occur in the supertemporal, not in history, and they exist apart from the temporal modality of reason.]

23. *Spirituality.* "Vollenhoven believed we could have knowledge of God, but that such depends on revelation. Dooyeweerd agrees that revelation is required, but his idea of revelation is much broader. Revelation or *'openbaring'* is the expression of a being from a higher ontical level to a lower. God reveals Himself from eternity to the created levels; humans reveal (*openbaar*) themselves by expression into the temporal realm. Without the idea of the supratemporal heart, we cannot understand God's revelation or Christ's incarnation. And we certainly cannot have the kind of spirituality that Kuyper describes in his meditations."[16]

Frame's Explanation of Reformational Philosophy

Frame begins his exposition of the Reformational philosophy in Section 4, "Common Sense and Science". Right away he identifies common sense and naïve experience, which, in turn, he wants to explain by Dooyeweerd's discussion of naïve experience in his lectures published as *In the Twilight of Western Thought*. Frame begins, then, confusing Dooyeweerd and Vollenhoven's ideas, simply calling this the "Amsterdam scheme". He then continues, "Dooyeweerd and the other Amsterdam thinkers clearly want to draw a *sharp* distinction between 'pre-theoretical' or 'naive' experience on the one hand, and 'theoretical' thought on the other. Sharp, that is, in the sense that every human thought must be classifiable, in principle, as *either "naive" or "theoretical"*. Frame goes on for a few pages trying to explain and also blow holes in this distinction. He relies heavily on J. M. Spier in his *Introduction to Christian Philosophy* (published by the Presbyterian and Reformed Publishing Company) and on Dooyeweerd's *Twilight* lectures. From what Frame quotes from Spier, he appears to be in the Vollenhoven camp, though nothing in Frame's booklet identifies that explicitly. Frame mixes the views of Dooyeweerd and Spier as though Spier were expounding Dooyeweerd.

But why are these theoretical and naïve thoughts distinct in Dooyeweerd's view? They are not just varieties of thoughts that we have while experiencing the world. Rather the naïve experience is

---

[16] J. Glenn Friesen, *Two Paths*, Appendix A, pp. 146-156.

John Frame's Critique of the Amsterdam Philosophy 13

where the experience emerges from the already existing supratemporal source and appears in the temporal, taking on the modalities that make up temporal experience. Once they pass into time the modalities separate, express their law structures, but lose their unity. Theoretical thought is a particular modality and here the naïve unity is lost, otherwise it would not belong to this modality. The initial naïve experience, though, is what indicates the supratemporal origin of experience.

But Vollenhoven had to give a different explanation, as he did not accept the supratemporal/temporal distinction. Here there would be something more like what Frame thinks he is criticizing, namely a distinction developing out of an original naïve experience. Nevertheless, even for Dooyeweerd there is something important for philosophical analysis at this point, for it is by "reflecting on" this first naïve experience that the philosopher catches sight, as it were, of the emergence of the modalities of temporal thought.

After this discussion, Frame concludes that, according to the Amsterdam view, "The 'opposition' between aspects which is distinctive of theoretical thought does not correspond to anything in the real world. The real world, rather, is that of naïve experience where the opposition does not exist." What does Frame take "real world" to mean here? For Dooyeweerd, only God has Being. That is one meaning of real. The created levels of supratemporal and temporal are creations of God. The supratemporal is where man's self is and in which the nuclear moments of all modalities of temporal experience also reside. Also, for Dooyeweerd the temporal preceded man in that it was already fallen when man was created. Nevertheless, the objects of temporal experience are individuality structures, and have no existence independent of the human mind. In that way, they are like Kant's phenomenal world. So where does Frame get his idea that the naïve experience is the real? He must be thinking in Vollenhoven mode.

But Frame uses this to try to construct a refutation. He says "in this scheme theoretical thought requires the use of premises derived from naïve experience," citing that "Dooyeweerd's writings include many references to God and the self, for instance, both of which are said be beyond all theoretical thought". He then argues that "If *a theory presupposes* propositions of a 'non-theoretical' kind, discusses those propositions, includes them in its theoretical structure, then what actually bars us from calling these propositions 'theoretical'?" Frame's problem is that he does not take into account the supratemporal. He is supposing that if something is not part of theoretical thought it must be part of naïve thought. And, then, if it is part of naïve thought, it must take the form of propositions. Finally, Frame takes "theoretical" in the normal sense of the word, so if there a body of propositions that theory makes use of, it is arbitrary and a misuse of language to insist that these are not themselves theoretical.

But for Dooyeweerd, everything religious is supratemporal (there is also the eternal). The self and its operations are in the supratemporal and propositions do not exist there. Propositions belong to the rational modality of the temporal. (Dooyeweerd does have an Ideas/concepts scheme, where Ideas are supratemporal and concepts temporal, something which Vollenhoven rejected.) How are these the propositions of theoretical thought if they are not propositions? For Dooyeweerd, the whole structure of the supratemporal, the self, the nuclear moments of the modalities, etc. are what produces temporal experience, and he calls that relation by the name of presupposition. The presupposition is that structure, beyond the access of the temporal modes of awareness, which nevertheless causes and accounts for the content of temporal awareness.

Now, of course, for Vollenhoven all of this must be different. If Frame was getting explanations from sources in the Vollenhoven school it would not fit with Dooyeweerd's system. Strangely, though, Frame immediately (Section 5) goes on to talk about the eternal and supratemporal in Dooyeweerd's thought, and to note that he "seems to imply that theoretical thought may not speak of anything eternal or supra-temporal." He then notes that Dooyeweerd nevertheless has much to say about these in his theoretical writings. Here Frame has a solid point, and it is the one that he should have made at the end of Section 4. Dooyeweerd did have some sort of theory about this, with recourse to a type of intuition that synthesizes things beyond the limits of the modality boundaries.

Frame, unfortunately, concocts his own explanation of what Dooyeweerd is doing.

> Essentially, he maintains that, while God and the self can be spoken of in a theoretical context, they have such special statuses in that context

that it is not quite proper to call them elements of the theory. That special status is that of *presupposition*.

To support this idea he quotes something from Dooyeweerd:

> ... All conceptual knowledge in its analytical and inter-modal synthetical character presupposes the human ego as its central reference-point, which consequently must be of a super-modal nature and is not capable of logical analysis.[17]

This is a reference to the synthetic intuition mentioned above. He notes that it operates outside the logical or rational modality, is a function of the central, supratemporal ego, and consequently is itself beyond the analysis of the rational temporal modality. This is all very Kantian. Our world is built by intuitive processes beyond our rational inspection. Frame misunderstands this as: "God and the self, Dooyeweerd is saying, are *presuppositions* of any true theory, and therefore not part of the theory itself."

But what is the specific character of Frame's misreading of Dooyeweerd? He is turning it into Van Tillianism. It was Van Til who would say that God was the presupposition of any true theory (he also said that God cannot be conceived of), and presuppositions connect them, but only by way of a move to a transcendental argument. Frame thinks that is the form that Dooyeweerd's thought also must follow. This confusion will show up again when Frame endorses Van Til's charge that Dooyeweerd's thought is autonomous thought, partly because he does *not* make God the presupposition.

From here Frame bumbles around about what a presupposition and central reference point are. He does not understand that the central reference point is not some sort of fulcrum, or anchoring point, of *a theory* being proposed, but the active supratemporal self, which transcends temporal experience and gives rise to it. And the content of this experience, recall, has no existence apart from the human knower. The central reference point, the supratemporal self, *makes it*. He then complains about how Dooyeweerd claims that we cannot have conceptual knowledge of God and self and then goes on to talk about both. Oddly, Van Til did the same thing. His objection to

---

[17] Cited from, Herman Dooyeweerd, "Cornelius Van Til and the Transcendental Critique of Theoretical Thought," in E. R. Geehan, ed. *Jerusalem and Athens* (Presbyterian and Reformed, 1971, p. 85.

Anselm's ontological argument is that it is invalid because we cannot conceive of God, yet Van Til had plenty to say about God. In Dooyeweerd's case, there was the distinction between Ideas (supratemporal) and concepts (temporal) which may be in play in this area.

Then Frame gets to a more interesting argument. He considers the implications for the truth of a theory that it cannot refer to the supratemporal, which is nevertheless essential to the theory. Unfortunately, he is still caught up in speaking of the "supra-temporal presuppositions of a theory" as though these were like premises, and how that makes for a relation in the theory which cannot be spoken of theoretically. What we need at this point is a theory of reference. Of course, something similar must occur in the problem of whether it is possible to refer to things-in-themselves in Kant's theory, and ample literature must exist on the question.

The same problem occurs for Van Til, although it arises in a different way. In his idealist theory of meaning, the meaning of things is the totality of relations that they have with everything else. As this knowledge is only available to God, only God has real knowledge, and men only have some approximation that arises from their limited experience. This is the reason why man's knowledge, for Van Til, can only be what he calls "analogical." But how, then, do terms outside man's experience have any meaning at all? What is not within experience, such as God, should not have a meaning, and reference to God should be impossible. All these theories face the same problem of how to climb out of what is essentially Kantian subjectivity.[18] As seen in (2) of the differences Friesen indicates between Vollenhoven and Dooyeweerd, for Vollenhoven creation does not refer beyond itself.

For Dooyeweerd, though, knowledge does not reduce to theoretical knowledge, because man's true self resides in the supra-temporal. There is a certain problem with it, as for Dooyeweerd the Fall is a fall of the temporal away from the supratemporal, so some loss of integration results from this. But the supratemporal is not absent either. The self and its intuitive operations still exist and function there. In fact, the intuitive integrative function mentioned twice already is going on there all the time. The question is whether and how

---

[18] Under this idealist interpretation of Kant.

this type of intuitive knowing connects to the concepts in theoretical thought.

In Section 6, Frame turns to Dooyeweerd's modes of temporal experience. He says that Dooyeweerd lists them according to ascending complexity. Now Friesen says that that is Vollenhoven's way of looking at it and that for Dooyeweerd the order is that in which the mode is distinguished in time. There is a relation between the modes and time, although it is not the one which Frame will try to explain a little further on.[19]

The various modes of temporal experience are listed and explained in an article by Magnus Verbrugge (Dooyeweerd's son-in-law). In his list, these are numerical, spatial, kinetic, physical, biotic, sensory, logical, and historical. There are longer lists. "None can be reduced to any of the others: each of them shows a certain sovereignty in its own sphere."[20] These have a definite order, which is irreversible, as each sphere depends on the preceding one. Frame comments that "This system is most impressive in its symmetry and balance, and if valid it provides a ready guide to the analysis of many problems in philosophy and other disciplines."

It would be interesting to know why Frame thought this. For ancient and medieval science a system of classification with clearly definable and necessary categories was the ideal. That is because, in the absence of understanding how things work, science was about classification and the order of knowing. Now, Dooyeweerd is pointing to something functional in his order of modalities, in that there is a dependence of the later ones on the earlier ones. But this is not a scientific classification or description, but an order in which these modalities have to be manifest in consciousness. As such, it has nothing to do with science in our modern sense. Verbrugge, in his article, clearly thinks that this is related to science in some fundamental way. After

---

[19] The emphasis on time is a feature of idealism in general. Time was important to Kant in discovering how the mind construes experience, it was a major theme for the 19th century theosophists, it was a problem for post-Kantian idealism, one which Van Til in his doctoral thesis pointed to as the principal reason to reject idealism as an explanation of reality, and appears in a decisive role in the Reformational philosophies as well.

[20] Magnus Verbrugge, "A New Look at Scientific Inquiry", *Contra Mundum*, No. 6, Winter 1993, pp. 16-17.

pointing out that Dooyeweerd distinguished naïve experience from theoretical knowledge, where science is, Verbrugge goes on to indicate the law-structures of the modal spheres as the area of scientific investigation. What is to be investigated are the "individuality structures". He objects to this term (from the English translation of the *New Critique*) as it suggests an individual entity. (This is also the idea one gets from reading Friesen's account.) Verbrugge prefers Roy Clouser's term "type-law". Here we are led to think of something like Thomistic forms (also understood by Thomas in terms of law). The key difference, however, is that these are products of the intuition within consciousness. Compare this to the approach of science that increasingly relies on mathematical models to represent a world, both on the subatomic and cosmological levels, that cannot be represented in an intuitive mental understanding, and has to be explored indirectly through complex experiments.

As an aside, Christian Reconstruction started along these lines, seeing itself as a development of Kuyperianism ("Kuyper plus the Bible") and guided by Dooyeweerd's philosophy. Rousas J. Rushdoony wrote the introduction to Dooyeweerd's *In the Twilight of Western Thought*,[21] (a series of lectures from an American tour, of which the "basic" material was prepared for publication by Henry Van Til) though without seeming to understand it very well, and published Verbrugge's book *Alive: The Origin and Meaning of Life*.[22] As late as 2004 Gary North distributed a proposal for a worldview course in which scientific law was to be presented as the modal spheres.[23] This is a regression to the pre-modern mentality. As a phenomenon, it is a much wider tendency than is found only in the neo-Calvinists, as a revival of Thomism shows a similar regression to the pre-scientific mind and its ideals of science.

Frame, despite admiring this classification, says that "the categories seem a bit arbitrary, a bit too easy, as if the world had to be squeezed a bit in order to fit the categories of the system." There follows considerable musing about what these modal spheres could be

---

[21] Herman Dooyeweerd, *In the Twilight of Western Thought* (Nutley, NJ: Craig Press, 1960).

[22] Magnus Verbrugge, *Alive: The Origin and Meaning of Life* (Vallecito, Calif.: Ross House Books, 1984).

[23] Gary North, "Biblical Worldview: An Outline", July 6, 2004.

and how they are identified. Yet he does not consider them in connection with Dooyeweerd's central point about the nature of philosophy. That is, philosophy begins with reflection on the emergence of experience via the naïve experience into the modalities, and attending to the way these appear.

For Dooyeweerd, these modalities come out of the supratemporal with their law-structures, which exist already in the supratemporal nuclear moment, and then are expressed in time. Frame thinks that it is time that creates these modalities; that they "are considered to be forms of time." Frame complains that there must be some equivocation on the meaning of time, and wonders "does 'supra-temporal' mean 'disordered'?" Had Frame started with the metaphysical system, and the analysis of reality into eternal, supratemporal, and temporal, he could have avoided his nearly random speculations and confusions.

When Frame finally turns to the model (Section 6, b) he resorts to ridicule.[24]

> Note again the rather heavy use of metaphor. The "center" in view is clearly not a geometrical center; the "starting point" is not a geographical starting point. The "concentration point" is not a piece of freeze-dried experience. What then do these phrases mean?

It is really not so difficult. The center is the functional center, also called the "self" where the intuition that creates conscious experience operates. There is a similar idea in Kant. The starting point is a functional origin. The concentration is the consequence of the idea of an original unity of experience. Surely Frame is not so uninformed about the philosophy of mind as not to be able to understand this! (But maybe so. Compare Van Til who refuses to disclose the philosophy of mind presumed by the mental operations in his epistemology. Could it be that it just never occurred to the Van Tillians that a philosophy of mind was necessary?) Frame continues:

> Does it mean that it is the heart which *has* all experiences? Does it mean that the heart furnishes the universal concepts by which experience is "unified" (i.e. organized, accounted for, analyzed, etc.)? Does it

---

[24] In a Preface added in 2005, Frame mentions that the "booklet also contains far too much smart-alacky stuff". This suggests that he would no longer take this line.

mean that all experience presupposes the existence of the heart? Does it mean that any true *account* of human experience must presuppose the existence of the heart? Does it mean that the heart somehow perceives supra-temporally what the senses perceive temporally?

All this is a refusal to attend to the account that Dooyeweerd actually gives. Frame simply refuses to take the supratemporal self seriously. But then, Vollenhoven did not believe in the supratemporal self, and we don't know how many of Frame's notions are coming from Vollenhoven's followers. As far as Frame's notes indicate, he depends almost entirely on Dooyeweerd's *Twilight* and writings of J. M. Spier. He needed a guide such as Friesen who would say plainly from the beginning that it is a matter of two, in important ways opposed, Reformational philosophies.

Frame next encounters the Reformational idea of religious. Recall that for Dooyeweerd, "religious" and "supratemporal" are synonyms. Frame quotes from Dooyeweerd "How could man direct himself toward eternal things, if eternity were not 'set in his heart'?" and from Spier: "If our heart were subject to temporality, we would not possess an idea of eternity and we would not be able to relate our temporal life to God in religious self-concentration." Frame counters, first, with the claim that this argument is *invalid*. "Would Dooyeweerd and Spier be willing to say that we could not have an idea of God unless we were God? Then why should they say that we must be eternal to have an idea of eternity?" Well, in point of fact, Friesen thinks that Dooyeweerd's nondualism is panentheism, so we *are* a part of God. But then Frame's reference to eternity shows that he does not understand the difference between eternity and the "created heaven" of the supratemporal. Dooyeweerd does not think that man is eternal. Frame's second point, though rather wild, is interesting and deserves a longer quotation.

> The argument is not only invalid, but *dangerous* as well. It is precisely this kind of argument which has been used throughout the history of thought to break down the creator-creature distinction. Over and over again, philosophers such as Plotinus, John Scotus Erigena, Thomas Aquinas and others have argued that we cannot truly know God or have relationships with God unless we share some sort of common being, some common attributes with Him. .... This sort of argument lies behind the "great chain of being" idea found in Greek philosophy (especially neo-Platonism), Gnosticism, and much current thought.

Next to this a quotation from Friesen is illuminating.

> Stellingwerff defines Gnosticism as the descent of the Divine to man and mysticism as the ascent to God, and finds both in Kuyper. In my view, both are an oversimplification. Gnosticism viewed the temporal world as something we need to escape from; Dooyeweerd (and Baader) opposed any spiritualistic flight. Koslowski has shown how Baader's theosophy was not Gnostic. Nor did Dooyeweerd believe in an identity with God; his mysdticism [sic] was that of panentheism, and participation in God.[25]

So while Frame got the argument wrong, thinking that Dooyeweerd said that the self is eternal, he did pick up on the direction where Dooyeweerd was going.

Frame next considers knowledge of God within the Reformational framework. "It is neither 'conceptual' theoretical knowledge, nor does it appear to be a form of naïve experience." Had Frame noticed it, he is answering his own objections to Spier's idea that man must relate to God in the supratemporal. Frame then notices that Dooyeweerd "objects strongly to Van Til's assertion that a Christian philosopher must submit to the 'thought-content' of Scripture. At times, this objection seems to rest on a misunderstanding of Van Til, namely, that Van Til is making the knowledge of God 'theoretical' in Dooyeweerd's narrow sense of 'theoretical'."

Let us be clear about this. Dooyeweerd had developed a model of the criticism of the thought of philosophies and cultures according to which they would take some one of the temporal modal spheres as the starting point of their explanation of things and in this way make it absolute, resulting in antinomies where things in other modal spheres were reduced to the basic explanatory modality. This way of doing things, of starting in the wrong place, was called by Dooyeweerd "autonomous thought." It disregards its true supratemporal origin. The different schemes according to which this was done he called the apostate Ground-motives. Of the three important ones, one was the scholastic nature/grace Ground-motive.

Van Til adopted this Ground-motive analysis as the method for his

---

[25] J. Glenn Friesen, *Two Paths*, p. 155, note 110. He is citing Johan Stellingwerff, *De VU na Kuyper* (Kampen: J.H. Kok, 1987) pp. 50, 53, and Peter Koslowski, *Philosophien der Offenbarung. Antiker Gnostizismus, Franz von Baader, Schelling*, (Vienna: Ferdinand Schöningh, 2001).

own apologetics, even while rejecting the model of supratemporal vs temporal spheres that it was based on. He discusses this in his class syllabus of 1954.[26] Of course, this presented a problem, because the Reformed dogmatics were developed using scholastic theology, as recent publications have been stressing.[27] Van Til wanted to arbitrarily refrain from applying his adopted method to his own tradition. So does Frame, in view of his comments about the "pretty arrogant" students at Westminster who pointed this out. Dooyeweerd indicated that Van Til himself was rationalist and scholastic in his method, according to this Ground-motive analysis. Amusingly, on the same page where Frame is complaining that Dooyeweerd criticized Van Til, Frame has a footnote where he criticizes a certain Peter J. Steen for not having "adequately purged himself of those 'remnants of scholasticism' which remain in his own thinking."

We can clarify matters by introducing the distinction of transcendence/immanence. Dooyeweerd characterized the philosophies built on apostate Ground-motives as immanence philosophies. Compared to what were they immanent and what transcended them? They were philosophies that explained things in terms of the temporal. They left out the supratemporal which transcends the temporal. In the same way the eternal transcends the supratemporal, so compared to both supratemporal and temporal the eternal is transcendent.

How does a philosophy succeed in climbing out of subjectivity to include the transcendent? According to Dooyeweerd we live in the transcendent, as the self is supratemporal and is the source of our temporal experience. There are two types of experience, supratemporal and temporal. The problem is that this supratemporal part is experienced in a non-theoretical way. Van Til claimed that there are two types of experience, revelation and the experience of the world. The problem is that as God's truth, meaning, and logic are inaccessi-

---

[26] Cornelius Van Til, *A Christian Theory of Knowledge* (Westminster Seminary syllabus, 1954) pp. 32, 33. See, also, *infra* p. 63.

[27] Eg. The various publications of Richard A. Muller, especially *Post-Reformation Reformed Dogmatics* (Grand Rapids: Baker Academic, various editions), Stephen J. Grabill, *Rediscovering the Natural Law in Reformed Theological Ethics* (Grand Rapids: Wm. B. Eerdmans Publishing Co, 2006), and J. V. Fesko, *Reforming Apologetics: Retrieving the Classical Reformed Approach to Defending the Faith* (Grand Rapids: Baker Academic, 2019).

ble because it requires an infinite mind to have them, revelation can only reach us in the immanence form of human language.

VAN TIL'S VIEW OF REVELATION AND LANGUAGE

Dooyeweerd said that revelation was experienced in the supratemporal, and left it there. It was therefore rationalist, autonomous thought to treat it as propositional and make a system of theological deductions from it. Van Til said that revelation was propositional (sort of) but, as it stood for God's thoughts and God's meanings as related by God's logic, it was rationalist, autonomous thought to make a system of theological deductions from it.

> We have repeatedly asserted that the facts of the universe are what they are because they express together the system of truth revealed in the Bible. But the point to note now is that what is meant by the idea of truth as found in Scripture does not mean a logically penetrable system. God alone knows himself and all the things of the created universe exhaustively. He has revealed himself to man. But he did not reveal himself exhaustively to man.... Man has not the capacity for such an exhaustive revelation. And God reveals himself to man according to man's ability to receive his revelation. All revelation is anthropomorphic.... Neither by logical reasoning nor by intuition can man do more than take to himself the revelation of God on the authority of God.... All the revelation of God points to the self-contained God. This God as self-contained makes every fact to be what it is. And therefore man's study of every fact, his understanding of any fact, is an understanding of something of the ways of God. Man's system of truth, even when formulated in direct and self-conscious subordination to the revelation of the system of truth contained in Scripture, is therefore not a deductive system. God has in himself absolute truth....
>
> But the main point to be emphasized here is that the system of truth as the Christian thinks of it as found in Scripture is an analogical system. To be faithful to the system of truth as found in Scripture one must not take one doctrine and deduce from it by means of syllogistic procedure what he thinks follows from it. One must rather gather together all the facts and all the teachings of Scripture and organize them as best as one can, always mindful of the fact that such ordering is the ordering of the revelation of God, who is never fully comprehensible to man.
>
> In the Westminster Confession of Faith the statement is made that that is true which by good and necessary consequence may be deduced

from Scripture. This should not be used as a justification for deductive exegesis.[28]

To understand this fully, it has to be taken with Van Til's theory of meaning. Van Til was trained as an Idealist, and there is no indication that he ever questioned the Idealist theory of meaning. The meaning of something is the totality of its relations with everything else. That fits with the Idealist anchoring everything in the Absolute. For Van Til, who could know the totality of the relations of things? Only God, and Van Til is explicit about substituting God for the Absolute in the place it holds for the explanation of reality.[29] Thus, while God has truth and meaning, this is not possible for man. What man has Van Til calls analogy. This is not only the case for the meaning of terms but for logic as well, which is not the same as God's logic. That is why it is impermissible to use logic in theology (except when it is). This problem, and Frame calls it a problem, is explained by him better than anyone else.[30] There is no criterion for when and when not to use logic.

When Van Til argues for his theory of analogy, saying that God does not reveal himself exhaustively to man, it seems like an evasion, as he is only stating what his dissenters agree on anyway, as though it affected the question of whether what God did reveal is true, and thus can be treated as truth in reasoning. But in Van Til's Idealist world, exhaustive knowledge is the only real or, as Van Til often calls it, absolute knowledge. From Van Til's perspective, this is germane to the argument, but he does not explain his Idealism, as it does not seem to occur to him that there is any other view.

In the present work, however, Frame says, "Doubtless the knowledge of God is more than the knowledge of verbal formulae, but it most certainly does not *exclude* such formulae. Doubtless, also, there is a sense in which God is incomprehensible, in which our knowl-

---

[28] Cornelius Van Til, *A Christian Theory of Knowledge* (Westminster Seminary syllabus, 1954), pp. 22, 23.

[29] It was a major point of his doctoral dissertation, where he attempted to show, by a transcendental argument, that God would fulfill the role where the Absolute failed, that is to account for the temporal nature of experience.

[30] John M. Frame, "The Problem of Theological Paradox", *Foundations of Christian Scholarship: Essays in the Van Til Perspective*, ed. Gary North (Vallecito, Calif: Ross House Books, 1976).

edge of Him is non-exhaustive; but Scripture always assumes that it is possible to have *true* knowledge of God which can be expressed in *true language*." Gordon Clark thought so too and for that Van Til had him run out of the Orthodox Presbyterian Church. Frame says, "We are not saying Dooyeweerd teaches the unknown God concept; but it is clear that he does not adequately guard against it." Ditto Van Til. What Van Til taught was that we have verbal revelation, but as we never quite know the meaning of the terms, we never quite know what propositions the verbal expressions assert. And even if we did, we would never quite know what they implied, so in that sense, we would not know the meaning either. So we have verbal, but not propositional revelation.

Section 7 is about **law**. As Dooyeweerd was professor of law and jurisprudence at the Free University, and not of philosophy, we need to ask whether law is meant in the sense of the law-structures of modal experience (which gave the philosophy the name of "Cosmonomic") or whether it means juridical law. I get the sense that Frame did not ask this question before he started writing about Dooyeweerd's view of law. He starts with the quotation that "Law is the boundary between God and the cosmos" which seems to suggest the modal concept, and proceeds to reflect on how God is above the laws but that they are "consistent with his character" so he would act according to them anyway. But Frame actually quotes the phrase from Spier. According to (3) in Friesen's list of major differences between Vollenhoven and Dooyeweerd, it was Vollenhoven who held this. Immediately after Frame expounds on how the modal laws regulate each sphere.

We can, of course, expect a problem in this area. The modal spheres are governed by law-structures which they acquire in the nuclear moment within the supratemporal. But one of the modal spheres is the jural. If that is temporal, it must be law in another sense. Frame speculates that "Law, like God and self, appears, first of all, to be a supra-temporal reality which is 'refracted' by the prism of time into a great diversity of specific precepts." What he seems to have in mind is that the law-structures of a modality acquire some detail within the particular modal sphere, and Verbrugge suggests that that is what science studies. Earlier we saw how Dooyeweerdians confuse the "laws" in the sense of the modalities of consciousness with scientific description of the physical world.

Frame then contrasts law in Dooyeweerd with law in the Bible, where he fails again to make distinctions. In the Bible, law is the Word of God, and the Word of God is God. Well, what about the law of gravity? Is that God? Frame says "The Law of God, in other words, is not some created machinery in the universe which mediates between God and man. The Law is spoken by God, not created by Him." Frame makes no effort to distinguish various meanings of law, either in his own mind or in Dooyeweerd's theory.

In Section 8 Frame takes up **Scripture**. Of course, it has not been possible to postpone the topic and it has come up before, but he can now address it in a more concentrated way. He says it is the most important topic. He adds, "Much is said in the literature about the radically scriptural character of this philosophy, and as we have indicated earlier, much of the initial appeal of this philosophy to Christians rests in its claim to relate Scripture to all areas of life." The very same can be said of Van Tillianism.[31]

Frame then describes the Ground-motive of Scripture, quoting from *Twilight*, the "radical and central, biblical theme of creation, fall into sin and redemption of Jesus Christ as the incarnate Word of God, in the communion of the Holy Spirit." He spends some time puzzling over what this can mean in the Reformational philosophy since it is not the ecclesiastical doctrines that are meant. Frame also wonders about the heart. This is distinct from the modal "faith aspect" in that the orientation of the heart affects everything, and the faith aspect is about cultic and ecclesiastical practices "attending church, engaging in prayer, or partaking of the sacraments." (He quotes this from Spier.)

The solution is really simple. The heart is another name for the supratemporal self, and creation, fall and redemption in the supratemporal are not the temporal events of the stories in Genesis. The temporal individuality structures have no existence apart from the human supratemporal knower, yet in Genesis creation of the world precedes creation of man. They are not the same thing.

There is, however, a further point that Frame wants to puzzle out.

---

[31] See, for example, Thomas Schultz, "VII: Presuppositionalism and Philosophy in the Academy", *Without Excuse: Scripture, Reason, and Presuppositional Apologetics*, ed. David Haines (Leesburg, Virginia: The Devenant Pess, 2020) p. 155.

For "some members of the Amsterdam school", he does not say which ones, Scripture "is a 'positivization' of *faith-norms* for a particular group of situations." This occurs in the faith-aspect modality. Frame is, of course, opposed to this restriction to the application of Scripture. "[W]e must reject the view that the Bible speaks directly only to this faith aspect. Scripture itself contains no hint of any such limitation in its relevance to human life." Frame follows with an incisive observation.

> Here is one of the surprising paradoxes of the Amsterdam philosophy. Many of us were first attracted to the movement by its promise to "open" the Scriptures, to show their relevance, not only to our Sunday "church" activities, but to all areas of our daily life. The more one studies the movement, however, the more one discovers the extent to which this philosophy "closes" the Scriptures, and the extent to which it really makes them a "Sunday" thing.

In trying to make sense of this, however, Frame can only draw comparison to neo-orthodoxy and its encounter theology, because Frame does not start with a metaphysical view of how the Reformational model is put together.

Frame's next objection to the positivization idea is that as a positivisation of the modal law-structure it "implies that Scripture contains nothing which could not, in principle, have been discovered through study of the law structure." Further, it is a time-bound positivization done by ancient man, and we have to do our own positivization.

In Section 9, on **philosophy and theology**, Frame first considers Dooyeweerd's complaint that the term "theology" is used ambiguously for either heart knowledge, or theoretical study of Church doctrine. Frame says that as he rejects the hard distinction between the two types of knowledge, he has no reason to restrict the term wholly into one category or the other. But the point is, that in light of Dooyeweerd's model of the knower, that is the consequence. If you reject the model, the consequence does not follow. Frame persists in thinking that these issues can be debated without taking into account the metaphysics of the situation of the knower. Instead, he thinks that this distinction in the idea of theology is the consequence of the "Amsterdam view of Scripture." Frame's approach can be compared to arguing against Kant's views on various points without taking into account Kant's distinction between the noumenal and the phenomenal and the limitations of phenomenal knowledge.

The same thing occurs in the idea of philosophy. Again, Frame says of "the Amsterdam view", without noting whether it is Dooyeweerd or Vollenhoven, "Philosophy is that science which shows the relations between all the other sciences. Philosophy gives a total worldview, showing the limits of human knowledge, showing the limits of each science, showing the general structure of the universe. The philosopher, therefore, has a right to tell the theologian what he may or may not do." But why? Because philosophy applies the metaphysical model, revealing where the various types of knowledge originate and what they are. Frame should understand this. Van Til was always talking about how Kant did this, that is, to apply a metaphysical framework to knowledge and how that made Christianity impossible, as long as what Van Til took to be Kant's basic premises were accepted. And then Van Til turned around and did the same thing, as we quoted above, telling the theologian that he may not construct a deductive theology from exegesis of Scripture *because that is not allowed in Van Til's idealist philosophy of meaning*. Once again, this use of a metaphysical model to restrict possible knowledge is the major and persistent criticism Van Til makes of 19th and 20th century philosophy and theology, and Van Til says it is a necessary consequence. Then Van Til practices the same move, though with a different model and different consequences, by applying his model to possible knowledge.

In Section 10 on **science**, Frame notices that this concept of science is philosophically driven, but instead of noticing that this creates an ancient and medieval (in fact Thomist-scholastic) view of science, he complains that it is not scripture-directed and brings up evolution as the only problem. Friesen says that Vollenhoven's philosophy is frequently used to defend creationist science, while Dooyeweerd repudiated creationist science.[32] Next, in Section 11 on **education**, he finds a big impact from the Reformation philosophy in its strong involvement in schools, and its opposition to confessional standards, in that such a commitment would mix the modal spheres of the faith-aspect with the analytic one pertaining to schools. This seems to be the main thing that triggered Frame to write his booklet.

This actually should not be an implication of Dooyeweerd's posi-

---

[32] Friesen, *Two Paths*, p. 132, note 104.

tion, because for him there exists the integrative intuition that relates the modal aspects, so they do not have to be separate in their operation. But it shows what the people who are attracted to the Reformational philosophy want to achieve by it, that is, they chose the consequence for reasons related to their ideas about education.

A similar issue arises about **church and society** (Section 12) where the church institution is sharply separated from other institutions where Christians function. Again, this is the sort of consequence that is drawn if people already want to go that direction and give the separation an ideological base. One could as easily build the opposite sort of theory. Frame misses a key point, however, that this playing off of the church institution versus other institutions misses the idea of the Kingdom entirely. The parallel to Meredith Kline and the Radical Two-Kingdom is striking, even though they would draw the boundaries between the common and cultic somewhat differently based on their covenant theory rather than modalities. For them, too, the Kingdom disappears to be replaced by the two pseudo-kingdoms of the common grace world and the institutional church.

The topic of **evangelism**, in Section 13, is much more complex. First Frame says that for Reformational thought the laws of the modal spheres are norms, and to break any of them, such as an aesthetic norm, is a sin against God. In his Section 7, on law, he had cited various statements by Spier. Frame interprets this as "Therefore it is 'sinful' to make an error in logic, or to use less than the most 'proper' English." Furthermore, the fall of man implies the apostasy of the whole temporal world. This matter is fraught with confusion. Friesen says that the fall of the temporal preceded the creation of man. But as creation, in that sense, is in the supratemporal, in what sense is there this before and after? The theosophical tradition that Dooyeweerd draws on sees man as created with a mission into the fallen temporal realm. The temporal, in falling, falls away from the supratemporal. This in some way involves man's fall, as it seems to alienate man's temporal experience from the supratemporal self in some manner. But man's fall is said to result from a wrong alignment of the will. As a result, man looses his proper root in the supratemporal, and needs to be re-rooted. This wrong rootedness appears in the temporal in man's theoretical endeavor in which he constructs his understanding beginning from a temporal modality instead of out the supratemporal.³³ Thinking of the Fall in sequential terms is a temporal way of conceiving of it, which becomes confusing when relating it to the supratemporal. God created the temporal, yet the individuality structures encountered in the temporal are the results of man's supratemporal self expressing itself into the temporal. Yet these individuality structures are related to the modal law-structures which have their nuclear moment in the supratemporal, and are in some sense also laws given by God. Are the laws also given in some way in God's creation of the temporal realm? Perhaps there is no account of how all this fits together.³⁴

The implication for evangelism indicated by Dooyeweerd, according to Frame, is that "the whole world is somehow involved in sin: rocks, trees, rivers; and especially corporate human entities such as families, schools, governments, etc." As these are all involved in sin, so must they all be in redemption as well. Evangelism then takes on the repair of all these things. Frame sees this as the failure to distinguish between sin and the effects of sin, as only persons can sin and

---

³³ In the theosophical tradition that preceded the Reformational Philosophy the time scheme was most developed in the thought of Franz Xaver von Baader (1765-1841). Baader was a Roman Catholic and, though originally a very successful engineer and chemist, became Professor of Philosophy and Speculative Theology at Munich. There were, for Baader, four levels concerning time: 1) the eternal, the uncreated place of the Being and Becoming of God where God was always actualizing new possibilities, 2) the supratemporal, created for intelligent creatures, the "created heaven" between time and eternity, which consists of the present, 3) the temporal, or earthly or cosmic, which has past and future time, but no present, and 4) the infratemporal, a false time with only the past and which is the realm of the demonic. The Fall entailed a falling away of the temporal from the supratemporal toward the infratemporal. This resulted in 1) a sort of alienation in time between the present and the past and future, and 2) the appearance of the demonic within the temporal. See: "Franz Xaver von Baader", *Encyclopedia Britanica*, 1911, https://theodora.com/encyclopedia/b/franz_xaver_von_baader.html, and Friesen, *Neo_Calvinism,* pp. 34-41.

³⁴ For an attempt to expound the relation of man, creation and the fall in a systematic way see the section "2. Primacy of Biblical myths on foundation or origin", in J. Glenn Friesen, "Imagination, Image of God and Wisdom of God:Theosophical Themes in Dooyeweerd's Philosophy ", pp. 42-51. https://www.academia.edu/66647014/Imagination_Image_of_God_and_Wisdom_of_God_Theosophical_Themes_in_Dooyeweerds_Philosophy?

be sinners, and he means an individual person, as organizations are excluded from the personal, in Frame's mind. The same applies to faith and repentance. Consequently, evangelism "is an exclusively personal category." Frame says it is dangerous to lose this personal focus to these concepts.

Evangelism raises the question of how the Reformational philosophy addresses the unbeliever and so also raises the topic of **apologetics**, where the philosophy engages with other philosophies. Here, in Section 14, Frame notes:

> Prof. Cornelius Van Til has for many years been considered by many to be in league with the Amsterdam school. Indeed, Van Til has supported the movement in many ways, endorsing much of the work of Dooyeweerd, Vollenhoven and the others. During the last several years, however, Van Til has become much more critical of the Amsterdam movement. Part of this change, indeed, has been due to the emergence of "younger radicals" within the movement such as Arnold De Graaff and Hendrik Mart. But part of it, too, has resulted from Van Til's closer re-reading of the writings of Dooyeweerd himself.

This period when Van Til supported the movement before announcing his criticism lasted about thirty-five years. The break came near the end of Van Til's career. Frame emphasizes the place of Dooyeweerd's transcendental reasoning in bringing about this break. This is a "critical inquiry into the *universally valid conditions, which alone make theoretical thought possible, and which are required by the immanent structure of this thought itself.*" (Dooyeweerd's words.) Van Til's own transcendental critique placed the "triune God of Scripture" as the only thing that could provide the necessary conditions. He objected to Dooyeweerd for coming up with something different, namely the scheme of temporal experience, a self that transcends time, and so on. Finally, the supratemporal, in turn, requires an origin, but Dooyeweerd does not permit going beyond this and saying the origin must be God. Van Til, as Frame reports it, thinks that this means that Dooyeweerd allows the autonomy of theoretical thought.

If we return to the transcendence/immanence distinction introduced earlier, Dooyeweerd calls autonomous thought the thought that takes its departure from the temporal, and not from the supratemporal, that transcends it. He also calls this an immanence philosophy. This is all based on Dooyeweerd's idea, or model, of the process of thought and experience. He does not include the eternal, as the human self and experience do not exist and take place there, so it is irrelevant to the issue of man's knowledge. Van Til insists that theoretical thought must take its starting point from God, and that to exclude what transcends the created is the real definition of autonomous thought.

Now, Dooyeweerd's definition is functional, in that it encompasses both areas where he thinks human experience functions, the supratemporal and the temporal. Van Til is not claiming that the human self exists in God and that human thinking starts in God (which would be the equivalent move), but only that the existence of God is the necessary explanation for the existence of human experience. Van Til and Dooyeweerd are thinking about this in different ways, and are not using "autonomous" in the same way either.[35] Perhaps Van Til never really grasped what Dooyeweerd meant. Frame doesn't get it either.

Frame adds that Van Til also made criticisms on some topics where Frame makes his own objections. These are, "the 'conceptual' *contentlessness* of Dooyeweerd's transcendental ground motives" (I think he means the creation, fall, and redemption scheme as being supratemporal) and the supratemporal self as the origin of experience. He might also have mentioned Dooyeweerd's view of Scripture. Frame concludes his discussion by summing up the failures of the Reformation philosophy under fourteen points.

---

[35] For further exploration of this confusion, see: Tim Wilder, *Theosophy, Van Til, and Bahnsen* (Rapid City: Via Moderna Books, 2023), where I argue that Van Til's and subsequent presuppositional thought is mired in confusion resulting from taking concepts from Dooyeweerd that do not work absent his model, and mixing in some assumptions from Van Til's idealist background, as well as later issues when Greg Bahnsen began to mix in analytic ideas about justified belief.

OTHER WRITINGS BY JOHN FRAME

The Tri-Perspectival Theology site, frame-pothress.org, has a file collecting several short articles by John Frame on the Reformational Philosophies. Under the general title of "Dooyeweerd and the Word of God", it mostly deals with Reformational views of revelation.

THE WORD OF GOD IN THE COSMONOMIC PHILOSOPHY

Frame deals with the topic in two parts.[36] The first part is headed "The Word as Event." Here he takes an angle much like that in his Section 8 on Scripture in his *Amsterdam Philosophy*. That is, he assimilates it to his understanding of neo-orthodoxy. We might compare these two views as responses to the impact of post-Kantian idealism.. Neo-orthodoxy drew on existentialism to focus on an "encounter", the "Christ-event", etc., and a personal but non-propositional revelation. This revelation was somehow in the Bible but was not the propositions of the Bible. With Reformational Philosophy we find an approach based on the phenomenology of experience, so that it is more philosophical. Yet it does not at all disdain the name "religious". There are some who prefer to find an emphasis on a more existential side of Dooyeweerd. For example, J. Glenn Friesen writes extensively about this, to the irritation of the "official" Dooyeweerdians who try to put an orthodox face on his philosophy.

What Frame first notes is a dualism between this existential heart engagement with revelation and the specific commands of Scripture about various aspects of life, "rules for this and that". Frame treats this as resulting in treating revelation as an *"event, a process."* But, we must remember that for Dooyeweerd revelation is supratemporal, so the terms "event" and "process" which we understand temporally are misleading in that context. Next Frame mentions an alternative char-

---

[36] The two parts originally appeared as a two-part article in *The Presbyterian Guardian*, Oct. 1972, pp. 124-125, and Nov. 1972, 140-142.

acterization of revelation as power. He objects to this emphasis, in that in the Bible revelation is language, and the effects of revelation, the "power", are the result of the language, that is the meanings. But this is not at all Dooyeweerd's sense of revelation, so the problem is not, as Frame constructs it, a matter of wrong emphasis within two aspects, but of talking about different things using the same term.

Frame comes closer to this in his next point, that "on the cosmonomic view" the "word" may not be "theoretically analyzed." He lists several points, essentially what he also says in the *Amsterdam Philosophy*, which are all to the effect of why this claim is unreasonable and implausible within Frame's world of propositional revelation. He either refuses, or does not recognize the need, to enter into the Reformational framework to deal with their idea of "revelation".

Frame next says that, even though the Reformational philosophy thinks that the word "cannot be theoretically analyzed, they do believe that it can be *characterized*", and then instances the "creation, fall into sin and redemption" scheme. This, recall, is one of Dooyeweerd's Ground-motives, and the one he thinks is the Biblical and correct one. But this is supratemporal, not events in history.

In the second part of his article, Frame turns to the "Forms of the Word". He here proposes to focus on the *media* of revelation: "the created world, prophets, apostles, written scripture." We should remind ourselves that, for Dooyeweerd, revelation is a being expressing itself from a higher level to a lower level. God expresses himself from the eternal to the created. This is what creation is. Because the created world is God's expression, then the theosophical perspective, that is to try to understand God from his expression in the cosmos, finds its support. Man, as image of God, expresses himself from the supratemporal into the temporal. This, too, is revelation.

Of the media, Frame says, these "are, after all, *created* things (except, presumably, Christ in his divine nature), and therefore point beyond themselves to God who speaks through them, and to other elements in the 'process'." Frame then explains that, as these forms of the word are part of the "word as event", then "in a real sense those forms *are* the word." But, for Dooyeweerd, in a real sense, we never experience anything other than revelation. As creation is God's expression, and expression is revelation, everything that can be experienced is revelation. Reformed thinkers are accustomed to thinking of God's revelation *in* nature. This is nature *as* the revelation.

Frame addresses this in terms of law-word in creation, saying what he also said in his *Amsterdam Philosophy*. He then turns to Scripture, about which he says that, as Scripture is an artifact in time and space, it can be studied theoretically. We must note that as Reformed thought has its general and special revelation categories, so Reformational thought has some kind of distinction between the sense in which everything is revelation, and the sense in which there is a Scriptural supratemporal revelation. The attempt to treat this in Frame's way as a temporal artifact to be studied *in order to deduce theology* is, for Dooyeweerd, scholasticism. Of course, there is the special theory of positivization, already discussed, which confines its use of Scripture to the faith modality.

In the main, this article merely repeats what is in the *Amsterdam Philosophy* booklet, and its utility is to get a restatement of some matters in case the other statement is not thought to be clear enough.

What is God's Word?

This is a summary of a paper from a conference that was an engagement with some Association for the Advancement of Christian Scholarship (AACS) people. It warns, "The summary has been made by the *Guardian*'s editor and he should be held responsible for any unfortunate expressions in it."

One such unfortunate expression is this. "But the Word in *Scripture is God come in human form;* it is an incarnation. The Bible is *both* Creator and creature, as Jesus is both God and man." This confuses the Bible with the incarnation.

In general, this paper expresses Frame's ideas, and does not address what he thought of the Reformation Philosophy, but is what he thought those people needed to hear.

Reply to Prof. Zylstra

Here Frame is responding to an article by Bernard Zylstra who was writing as a member of the (AACS). Though not dated, Frame mentions that at this point he has been making criticisms of it for four or five years. Again the issue of Frame's understanding of the movement surfaces: "my arguments were met with Gnostic replies ("you don't understand") and even gratuitous attacks on my character." Frame discusses Zylstra's article under three heads.

The first is the relation of law to God. He leads with a quotation from Zylstra.

> In this booklet Frame asks the fundamental question: What is the relation of law to God? Before he answers this question he formulates the frame of reference within which the answer can be given: "The Scriptures teach that God is creator, the world is his creature, and that there is nothing in between, no third category." (p. 29). Here, we submit, Frame departs from the teaching of the Bible, which clearly posits a "third category", namely the Creator's law for creation, the statutes, ordinances, and words that creature must obey and do. The absence of this "third category" in Frame's conception makes it extremely difficult for him to understand the bible on this score, as we will see later.

What is very striking about Frame's discussion of law in his *Amsterdam Philosophy* is the very simplistic and biblicist nature of his approach. And this is not only due to his ignoring some aspects of Reformational theory, as Christian theology had long debated how to understand God's law in terms of his creation order. The relation of God's sovereign freedom, the ordained order in creation, and God's prescriptive will was debated from the eleventh century up through the Puritan theologian William Ames, and this discussion is analyzed in the works of the medievalist Francis Oakley. By no means are these views reducible to those of Thomas Aquinas. A summary of Oakley's history is in Appendix I of *Divided Knowledge: Van Til & Traditional Apologetics*.[37] Frame perhaps thinks that Van Til has swept away all such philosophical and theological reflection and also the need for it. Others (e.g. Gary North) thought that Van Til left a gaping hole in his thought in the area of law. Frame's attempt to slide over the matter, by saying that law is simply God speaking, seems a shocking reduction.

Frame, for once, takes a metaphysical view and says that there is God, creation, and nothing else. So anything, e.g. law, must be one or the other.

> Now what about "law"? Is law creator or creature? Well, that's easy, isn't it? Law is that word of God by which all things were made (Gen. 1:3, Psm. 33:6, John 1:1-3, Heb. 11:3, II Pet. 3:5). The law has divine attributes (Ps. 19:4-9, 119:89, 160, etc.) To obey law is to obey God; to

---

[37] Tim Wilder, *Divided Knowledge: Van Til Traditional Apologetics* (Rapid City: Via Moderna Books, 2023).

disobey law is to disobey God. God's law, God's Word, is God Himself (John 1:1).

So what are all those Mosaic ordinances? There are commands to do ritual purifications, sacrifices, fasts, etc. Are these commandments God? If God does not change, how can these commandments change? The silliness of Frame's proposal is evident. Of course, if he were to give a different answer he would have nine hundred years of arguments and distinctions to take into account. But Frame insists that any other answer than his creates a semi-divine mediator between God and man.

There is a theological tradition that goes in this direction. It sees justice only truly realized in God and only manifest on earth in Christ, and only achieved eschatologically. This is Barthian Christocentrism, and an instance of this (following a lengthy analysis of law itself) is in Jacques Ellul's *The Theological Foundation of Law*.[38] This seems to be the option open for theological development from Frame's position, but of course not one that he would be prepared to take.

The shortcomings of Frame's position do not imply that Zylstra is right in making an ontological third category. He seems to have fallen into a linguistic trap by not considering what he was saying. Zylstra is taking law in a very wide sense including the laws for creation as well as God's commandments. Now, if the law is God, and if this wide sense of law is accepted by Frame, as it appears to be, then the present form of creation expresses God's nature, not his free choice, and is itself necessary. This is the view of Averroes, which the medievals, at least, regarded as heretical. (I have argued that Van Tillians tend in this Averroest direction.[39] It is inherent in the way their transcendental argument works out, as the characteristics of the world must require something in God that accounts for them. This was a point of difference between Van Til and Dooyeweerd, according to whom transcendental reasoning cannot get beyond the idea of Origin.)

---

[38] Jacques Ellul, *The Theological Foundation of Law*, trans. Marguerite Wieser (New York: Seabury Press, 1969). Available online.

[39] Tim Wilder, *Theosophy, Van Til, and Bahnsen* (Rapid City: Via Moderna Books, 2023) p. 93.

Under the second head, Frame says

> "word of God" in the Bible may be understood as a kind of "linguistic communication." Professor Zylstra thinks that this is a "reductionist" view. I must say that I am entirely baffled. What is a "word"? A word is a "linguistic communication." "Word" and "linguistic communication" are synonyms

Frame has just come off of saying that law is Word is God. Now he says it is a synonym for linguistic communication. If we return to the previous "What is God's Word?" article, under point 2 we find this

> The Word is not only identified with God, it is distinguished from God (John 1:2). It is *by* the Word that the heavens were made, so that the Word is a tool. There is a unity *and* a distinction which we cannot account for.

> There is a mystery here like that of the Trinity, the one God in three persons.

So (remembering that this was the editor's summary) we find Frame saying that Word in the Bible is a synonym for linguistic communication *and* that it is a deep mystery like the Trinity. No wonder Zylstra thought Frame was being reductionist in the former case.

But Zylstra was basing his view on his own arguments, some of them silly, as Frame says, but also that God's word is his decree that governs and upholds all things. Frame replies with his own silly argument that it cannot be said that power is more than language because a president can declare war. For proof that Frame came to understand much more than this, see his discussion in *The Escondido Theology*, pp. 237-241.

The third head is where Frame points out that he does not consider the Word of God to be only the Bible. This is something he says he must keep repeating to the Reformational people because the don't seem to hear it.

Toronto, Reformed Orthodoxy, and the Word of God: Where Do We Go from Here?

The last of these short articles is about an aspect of the debate that should be very interesting but is seldom directly addressed. Frame makes a clear statement of a phenomenon, in which this aspect makes its appearance.

> My present bafflement chiefly derives from a rather paradoxical feature of the "Toronto approach." On the one hand, the rhetoric of the movement suggests that the AACS is urging upon the church an exciting, new view of the Word of God, a view which, though taught in Scripture itself, has been buried under centuries of rationalistic, scholastic, nature-grace dichotomizing theology and has recently been rediscovered through the monumental intellectual energies of Dooyeweerd and his disciples, thus liberating the Christian community from the shackles of the past. On this view, the contemporary villains are the orthodox Reformed theologians who do not appreciate these great AACS rediscoveries and thus are perpetuating a traditionalism which in the present context is counter-reformational. Such rhetoric fires the hearts of young zealots. Students go off to weekend conferences and come back prepared to subject the whole theological tradition to a "radical transcendental critique." Their ministers, parents, and seminary professors, of course, are incapable of understanding these new insights: how could they possibly understand, caught up as they are in the chains of nature-grace thinking?

> On the other hand, on at least three different occasions when I have presented what I considered to be sharp criticisms of the Toronto approach and have presented my own positive view (which I consider fairly traditional), I have been told by rather prominent AACS people (Peter J. Steen, James Olthuis, Paul G. Scrotenboer) that my views did not differ substantially from theirs, that in fact they "agreed" with me.

Frame says "Despite your professions of 'agreement' with me, I still suspect that we disagree on some pretty important matters." There is, of course, one clear explanation that I have relied on in my discussion. That is that Dooyeweerd developed a metaphysical model that differs from orthodox Christianity so radically that people just could not grasp it. The reason is that it went far beyond what they could imagine could come out of the Free University and from Neo-Calvinism. As people like Frame kept responding to what they constructed as their own more reasonable view of the philosophy, the other side saw that they kept missing the point.

So why did not the Reformational side clarify matters? I think the answer must lie in two directions, neither of which is very "nice". One is that like modern French philosophy, Canadian Reformed theology, and similar movements, obscurity and obfuscation are part of the philosophy. It is a mystification that is essential. This always comes with a certain amount of posturing. The spokesmen for the movement "can't understand why they are misunderstood" and when any criticisms are based on the logical implications of the philosophy, then the spokesmen "don't recognize themselves in these criticisms". The other answer is that if people catch on to everything, then away go the jobs in confessional organizations, the donations, and the influence.

The rest of Frame's article is his restatement of his position on Scripture, this time pointing out many specific points where he thinks this differs from what the Reformational people are saying or from the implications of what they are saying. Frame still does not understand why they differ, only in what they differ, but he does know that what he has to say here is the historical protestant view.

REPORT BY CORY GRESS ON REFORMATIONAL PHILOSOPHY

Frame's *Critique of Reformational Philosophy* has been paired with a critical essay by Cory Gress in the Spanish language edition published in Mexico.[40] Titled "A Report From the Desert", it in some ways makes an odd combination. Gress is a pastor in the Protestant Reformed Church (PRC), trained in their seminary. The PRC broke away from the Christian Reformed Church over their adoption of Common Grace theology as official church dogma. The PRC opposes the Common Grace teaching root and branch. Van Til's theology and philosophy made up an ideology that was Common Grace to the core, and John Frame followed Van Til as the standard bearer for Van Tillianism, until the current champion, K. Scott Oliphint, took over at Westminster. Gress sees the Reformational philosophy as a phenomenon that is general to the Dutch Reformed denominations, with very bad effects, and he wishes to bring attention to the problem.

Gress defines Reformational philosophy as "a movement within the stream of neocalvinism to establish a Christian Philosophy".[41] He says that the Reformed Church in America (RCA) and the Christian Reformed Church have been the home of this philosophy from its beginning, and he points out the liberal direction in which these denominations are headed. I would have said that they have long since arrived. Gress says nothing about that Mecca of weirdness, the Canadian Reformed Churches. Gress points to the acceptance of homosexuality, homosexual "marriage", women in church office, and then the combination of the two with lesbian ministers in the RCA.

Gress then claims that Nicholas Wolsterstorff (called "Dr.

---

[40] Cory Gress, "Un reporte desde el desierto," *Crítica a la Filosofía Reformacional* (Villamermosa, Tabasco: Reforma Press, no date). I am working from this Spanish translation.

[41] Gress, p. 133, note 93.

Nicholaus Woltersdorf" one place in the text) "a noted reformational philosopher at Calvin College" gave a lecture supporting homosexual marriage.[42] The problem is that Wolsterstorff, who has moved on to Yale, is not a Reformational philosopher. He is, in fact, pretty much the opposite. The Wikipedia summary of his views says:

> Wolterstorff builds upon the ideas of the Scottish common-sense philosopher Thomas Reid, who approached knowledge "from the bottom-up". Instead of reasoning about transcendental conditions of knowledge, Wolterstorff suggests that knowledge and our knowing faculties are not the subject of our research but have to be seen as its starting point. He rejects classical foundationalism and instead sees knowledge as based upon insights in reality which are direct and indubitable. In *Justice in Love,* he rejects fundamentalist notions of Christianity that hold to the necessity of the penal substitutionary atonement and justification by faith alone.

Almost every point in this description of his philosophy is a rejection of a major point of Dooyeweerdianism (and also Van Tillianism). Of course, "fundamentalist" in the quotation is the snide liberal way of saying "historical Protestant".

Continuing with his disclosures about the two Reformed denominations, Gress points out that they and their colleges are compromised with an evolutionary view of human origins, and then mentions Wolterstorff again as teaching that Jews and Muslims worship the same God as we do, but in a different manner.

Gress then asks the reason for this and says that there is more than one answer, but part of it is the influence of Reformational thought in these denominations. If Reformational thought is part of the answer, what was the rest of the answer? If we are to blame Reformational thought it would seem to be important to see its relative place among the other influences that brought about these changes and also to see where there was some synergism between these influences.

At the time that these influences were being noticed and accepted in the Christian Reformed Church, I happened to be a reader of the opposition press that was reporting on the progress of liberalism in the denomination. Most notable was the campaign to have women elders and the reasons for it. How this was conducted, on both sides,

---

[42] Gress, p. 136.

is very instructive. The campaign for woman elders was waged based on the ideology of the movement for women priests in Roman Catholicism and high church Episcopalianism. The feminists insisted that women could perform the same role as men in, for example, "imaging Christ" to the congregation. There was really no interest, at the ideological level, in having women as Reformed elders, but rather the issue was argued in terms of the high church priestcraft. At the local level, however, I saw something different. Here the women pointed out that the men did not want to be elders, anyway, because of the burden of all the work involved, while they did want the job. But when the women got into leadership, what they wanted was to get up in front of the congregation and be seen, and change the tone of everything with their performances. The Reformational theology in this process was represented by very few people, nobody understood it anyway, and it was not influencing decisions. (The exception may have been in Norman Shepherd's own congregation, where there was a vocal Reformational presence.)

Another influence was New Age theology. Again, it was something that appealed to women, based on affirming female religiosity and making a change away from Reformed ideas and practices. The women wanted a change in religion in doctrine, practice, and style. They were fed up with the old model.

Where Reformational theory was being voiced was mostly in association with science. Coming from Canada, the Reformational (in the Vollenhoven tradition) people were saying that the Holy Spirit was teaching us, through his *other* book of revelation, namely science, that new ideas of human origin, child raising, and political and judicial organization and norms were now the truths to be accepted. Even in this area, they were not alone, as at Calvin College there was Howard J. Van Till who argued a view of revelation that was essentially the same as that of C. S. Lewis, and tried to separate the vehicle of Scripture from its religious message. On this basis, he thought it did not matter to theology if, not just Genesis, but everything up through the time of David (based on his examples; he did not say it stopped there) was just folk tales with a religious message.

Over against this, the opposition, as far as I could see, was made up of two groups. One was the lay people fighting the culture war on particular issues that came up in their local area and the other was the church theologians. These church theologians – the two notable examples were Norman Shepherd and Robert Godfrey – were arguing the narrow exegetical case against women elders, etc. Only the conservatives cared about Biblical authority. It was not effective with the rest of the church people, who wanted change for other reasons. Ignoring the new religious mentality that was behind the changes was not going to do anything. These conservatives could not see that ignoring the agenda of the advocates of change, who did not care about the semantic range of Greek words, was not fighting the battle. Shepherd, of course, was famous for his deviation from Reformed theology on the doctrine of justification, and Godfrey showed his hand when he later presided over the takeover of Westminster Seminary, California by the Radical Two-Kingdom theology faction. Both were professors of churchianity unsuited to fight the cultural battles.

But Gress wants to argue that there is something intrinsic in Reformational philosophy that takes the church in this direction. First, he argues the distance of this philosophy from Calvin. He points out the role of Abraham Kuyper and neo-Calvinism. On top of this, Dooyeweerd brought a different view of the Scriptures, that is he lowered it, and elevated the place of philosophy, that is, of its own importance.

Gress wants to make clear that he does not have the perspective of an anabaptist or desire flight from the world. Rather he wants to live in all areas of life in a Christian way, and to have this taught to the people. And he agrees with the Dooyeweerdians that there is no neutrality. Success, though, depends on divine Providence and this "influence" waxes and wanes. In any case, Christ gathers his church and builds his kingdom. How far he really means it becomes clear later when he launches his attack on postmillennialism. He seems to have the standard PRC attitude where living out the Reformed faith becomes a matter of formulas and moralisms in the faith aspect, plus Christian schools, more to evade culture than to affect it.[43]

Grees then describes the modal spheres and their laws. These laws

---

[43] It is instructive to read old issues of the PRC's publication, *The Standard Bearer*, where editorials expose the shocking developments at Calvin College where there was interest in culture in the form of the arts, and the students even performed dramas! The name, ironically, goes back to Kuyper's *De Standaard*, and reflects the denominational origins out of Dutch neo-Calvinism.

or norms, according to Dooyeweerd, are the word of God, just as the Scriptures are the word of God. In fact, the Scriptures are only a part of this more fundamental word of God. The Scriptures are the word of God with authority only for one modal sphere. They are not intentional declarations of truth outside of the faith aspect.[44] For example, the days of Genesis do not have anything to do with 24 hour periods because Scripture is concerned only with the faith aspect.

Gress characterizes this as not using Scriptures as a definite truth, as a lens through which to view life, but as a vague inspiration about life. This, he says, leads the Reformational philosophers to put philosophy above theology, and to criticize systematic theology. But, in fact, Gress says, we must know something intentionally (*"propositivamente"*, but see the note below) to be Christians. Dooyeweerd calls dogmatic theology, which establishes the content of Scripture in propositions, "dangerous". But, in fact, Gress says, the Scriptures have a system of rational and coherent thought and to deny this is to deny the Scriptures. He cites Dooyeweerd's *Twilight*. But as this was published in 1960, why did it take Van Til and others at Westminster Seminary another decade to break with this teaching? Doesn't this show that if Gress is not exactly barking up the wrong tree, he is ignoring the grove?

His next point is that the unifying area of thought, for example in universities, formerly was theology. But now Reformational thought puts theology in a corner and gives its former place to philosophy.[45] This leads to setting aside the authority of Scripture as well. Reformational thought says the moral law is found more fundamentally in creation. Isn't this, though, the vision that Robert Godfrey made dominant at Westminster, California? It is natural law that is determinative for life, outside of the faith aspect.

But Westminster, California was heavily influenced by the Biblical Theology of Meredith Kline. Is there a connection to Reformational

---

[44] The Spanish text says *"declaraciones propositivas de la verdad"*, which means "declarations of resolve of the truth", but I am not confident that the translation, here and in the next paragraph, was correct. Perhaps "propositional declarations" was meant.

[45] With the current surge in the popularity of Thomism, it is important to consider how far it does the same thing in the form of philosophical theology.

philosophy? Nobody says there is, but we can notice a broad similarity.[46] Both speak of a created heaven. In Kline, this becomes the Upper Register, which the cosmic pulls away from in some manner in the fall so that the created heaven has a continuing but unperceived presence. For Dooyeweerd, of course, the created heaven is also called the supratemporal. True religion from then on involves restoring the proper relation between our existence in the temporal and the reality of the created heaven. The practical application to temporal life outside of the faith aspect is also similar.

The next section of Gress's essay introduces example statements of various Reformational philosophers. Unfortunately, again the first example is Wolterstorff, who is not a Reformational philosopher. Next is "Reformational theologian" James Olthuis, who is quoted from an article by William Dennison, "Dutch Neo-Calvinism and the Roots for Transformation: An Introductory Essay."[47] Superficial and inaccurate, the article is nevertheless interesting in that it describes a type of neo-Calvinism, distinct from what he calls the creation-order type. This is the "shalom neo-Calvinists" among whom he places Wolterstorff. He even quotes a bit of Wolterstorff's criticism of Dooyeweerd. Dennison then notes, "Wolterstorff admits that shalom is a synthesis of certain positive traits from Reformed Kuyperianism and Christian Marxism (liberation theology)".[48] But it is not Reformational philosophy.

An important point that Gress does pick up on from Dennison is the adaptation by the shalom-order neo-Calvinists of the theology of the nineteenth-century Dutch Kuyperians to their social vision. As Dennison points out, this was democratic socialism, and in that way

---

[46] Kine does acknowledge a debt to "cosmonomic philosophy", but objects to what he sees as a "neo-Dooyeweerdian" rigidity in that that modalities do not allow God to make structural adjustments in the course of the redemptive program. He also objected to "the neo-Dooyeweedian assumption that all creation can be identified in monistic fashion with the kingdom-realm of God". Meredith G. Kline, *Kingdom Prologue: Genesis Foundations for a Covenantal Worldview* (Eugene, Or.: Wipf & Stock, 2006), pp. 170, 171.

[47] https://the-highway.com/neo-calvinism.pdf, p. 287. Taken from *JETS*, 42/2 (June 1999).

[48] Dennison, p. 284.

there is continuity with the shalom-order neo-Calvinists of today.[49] This eschatological aspect of neo-Calvinism does not sit well with Gress's Protestant Reformed pessimillenialism. In the hands of Reformational thinkers, sanctification turns into cultural transformation. Another doctrine warped by Reformational thought is election.

Gress then issues a call for a return to Biblical authority and teaching in the church and for genuine Christian education on that basis.

My main problem with Gress's analysis of the Reformation theology is that he gets cause and effect backward. Reformation philosophy is a speculative philosophy about the nature and origin of phenomenological experience. Its flaws stem partly from its very un-biblical model of man, the world, and their relation to God, but its application is not determined by the underlying philosophy, which could be constructed to support almost any view. Rather, the Reformational philosophers apply it on behalf of what they already believe. Reformational philosophy is not the cause of the problems in the Reformed denominations, but it is put in the service of the deviations from orthodoxy, just as the other philosophies and theologies of these liberals are employed. It would not matter whether they held to Reformational philosophy, shalom neo-Calvinism, Thomism, process theology, or anything else, even Kuyperianism. In the hands of these people, any of these would be found to support the same outcomes. We are, of course, long past this point. Most of these viewpoints are themselves now being attacked from the "woke" perspective, and the only one that stands much of a chance of passing is the "shalom" type, which could be characterized as early-woke.

We already explained above how Reformational philosophy postures as a philosophy of science when it is nothing of the sort, as it is not about the world that science explains but about the appearance of phenomena in subjective experience. Neither does it provide views of society or institutional arrangements, but for that reason does not refute the ones that the adherents layer onto it. What it does do, however, is remove Biblical authority. But we have also noted that practically speaking Van Tillianism ends up in the same place.

---

[49] Dennison, p. 287.

REPLY BY ALDOLFO GARCÍA DE LA SIENRA

Fifty years ago John Frame wrote his critique of the Reformational Philosophy as a practical response to the aggressive and disruptive activities of the adherents of this philosophy. This was partly the actions of students at his seminary, where, frankly, the faculty had it coming, but mostly it was the efforts of the Reformational Philosophy zealots to block the establishment of distinctively Christian schools or other institutions and to oppose the activities of Churches and parachurch organizations that did not conduct their activities in the manner required by the Reformational thought.

Now a Mexican scholar, Adolfo García de la Sienra, has published a reply to Frame because he says that Frame's book "has been used as a battle horse in Mexico by people unwilling to seriously study the WdW, let alone argue rationally."[50] His preferred name for the movement is the philosophy of the Law-Idea, which he abbreviates from the Dutch as WdW, though he says it is commonly (in Spanish he says vulgarly) called "reformational philosophy". The prevalence of the latter name, though, is because it is the one that the Vollenhoven branch likes to use of itself and they are spread internationally and institutionally to the extent that they set the pattern.

García immediately goes to the point that "Frame quotes authors who disagree with its principal author, Herman Dooyeweerd, instead of sticking to what he states. This is a bad tactic in philosophy." This is the same point that I made over and over in my discussion of Frame's book, but Frame did not know this. He was under the impression that there was only one Reformational Philosophy. García preserves a total silence about this, as though there was only at first the philosophy of Dooyeweerd and later some disciples who differed on some points. In fact, his suggestion that Herman Dooyeweerd

---

[50] Adolfo García de la Sienra, *Philosophy and Reformed Theology: Response to John M. Frame's* The Amsterdam Philosophy, trans. Steve Martens (Niagara, Onterio: Cántaro Publications, 2024) p. 47.

was the principal author ignores the fact that, from the beginning, Vollenhoven was actively creating a significantly different philosophy, and, in fact, of the two it was Vollenhoven who was the philosophy professor at the Free University. Why García won't talk about this one can only speculate.

He then launches into the idea of the philosophical prolegomenon to theology. He discusses the history of this, noting that for a long time in the Netherlands it was based on the Jesuit Suárez. He then mentions modern theology, Karl Barth, and then jumps to Scotland, James Orr, and, oddly, Gordon Haddon Clark and Ronald Nash. Here he says, "the philosophical positions of these thinkers should be studied in a Presbyterian reformed seminary and should be discussed rationally." Is this a dig at the Van Tillians at Westminster because he knows how they have abused these writers? Anyway, I would not agree with García on this point because Clark and Nash simply are not important enough or complete enough.

Immediately García continues, "Synods (such as the Synod of Dort) are responsible for discussing confessions of faith, not the prolegomena to theology." And why not, as the prolegomena will to an important extent determine the theology? Is this perhaps an application of some Reformational modalism where certain institutions may only address the faith modality and not the analytical modality?

He concludes this section by mentioning the irony that "some Presbyterians have waged war against the first school in the history of Western philosophy that explicitly wants to presuppose the biblical religious motive."[51] Well, this idea of a religious motive is an aspect of the Reformation philosophy itself, and whether it is any good depends on the validity of the philosophy. When García gets around to trying to define it, he admits that the idea of a religious motive is very difficult and struggles for a couple of pages with it.

I think the problem is partly of his own making. As I have noted, Dooyeweerd liked to use paired religious and philosophical terms, so he could come at topics from either direction and it also works out that the religious term in the pair is more ambiguous and confusing. "Religious motive" is the pair to the term "Ground-motive". This is the aspect of Dooyeweerd's thought that most delighted Van Til. In

---

[51] García, *Response*, p. 50.

the next section, I will explain why I think that this is bad philosophy and history.

Then García says that Frame "seems to think" that this need for a prolegomenon implies "that the philosopher has the right to tell the theologian what Scripture can and cannot say." The reason he thought that this was Dooyeweerd's position is that it was what Dooyeweerd thought. He castigated Groen van Prinsterer, Abraham Kuyper, and Van Til for trying to construct their theology from the exegesis of Scripture.[52] García goes on to claim that Dooyeweerd taught the opposite of what Frame concluded, in that "Scripture speaks to the common man *without the mediation of philosophy* (or theology)." But what do the Scriptures speak to such a man? We turn to J. Glenn Friesen for his explanation.

> Dooyeweerd is adamant that the meaning of the meaning of creation, fall, redemption, sin, rebirth or even the meaning of the supratemporal heart is not to be determined by exegesis of the Bible. The Bible does not speak of creation, man's fall into sin, redemption, or rebirth in conceptual terms.... On what other basis do we form our theology? For Dooyeweerd, the answer is our experience....
>
> The Scriptures speak to our supratemporal heart, but they are not to be understood in a propositional way.... The Christian Ground-motive of creation, fall and redemption cannot be determined by theological exegesis.[53]

Is it any wonder that Frame tended to understand Reformational ideas through the model of Neo-orthodoxy, the other theology that spoke this way?

García glosses this as "the knowledge provided by Scripture is not a theory (neither philosophical nor scientific)." It is not a theory because it is not propositional for Dooyeweerd. "Precisely what the WdW defends is that philosophy must be subject to Scripture!" But it is not the propositions of Scripture but the philosophically constructed Scripture!

The next topic is the nature of the theoretical. Frame in his booklet gave a lot of space to jousting with the Reformational philosophy

---

[52] See Friesen's discussion of Dooyeweerd's ideas about this in his *Neo-Calvinism*, pp. 387-389.

[53] Friesen, *Neo-Calvinism*, p. 390.

over the naive/theoretical distinction and the definition of the theoretical. He thought the distinction was too sharp. I passed rapidly over this because it seemed to me that Frame had missed the underlying model of eternal/supratemporal/temporal and that his arguments were largely beside the point. Of course, he was sometimes engaged against those who did not accept this model, which Vollenhoven had rejected. García gets into his theory of science which is of models with a shared axiomatic structure. He begins to suggest an idea, that he will return to, that scientific investigation supports the modality-analysis of the world.

What Frame thinks is that the theoretical is an organized treatment of propositions and that, as the Reformational philosophers write sentences about all sorts of topics and that such sentences have no purpose except to express propositions, then Scripture, the supratemporal, theology, etc. are all the material of the theoretical. When Dooyeweerd or the others say that they aren't, Frame begins to speculate on what they could possibly mean by such strange claims, since on the face of it their discussion of these matters is theoretical! But Frame's speculations lead to wrong ideas of the Reformational Philosophy and when he makes conclusions from the wrong ideas he gets himself into trouble.

This leads right into Frame's problems with sphere-laws. Frame thinks that Dooyeweerd believed that the modalities were aspects of time. In fact, he quotes directly from Dooyeweerd that they are "aspects of time itself."[54] The idea that everything is time he finds very problematic in that "this view seems to rest upon an equivocation in the use of 'time' which has no basis in the actual meaning of the word." Frame cannot get past beating the air because once again he leaves out the basic model. For Frame, time must have to do with sequence and duration.

García goes into the history of rationalism, with its logicist program of building mathematics out of logic, and then points to the explosion of this idea in Gödel's demonstration of the incompleteness of second-order logic. This is supposed to show the independence of the modal spheres.[55] Here García begins to introduce an-

---

[54] Dooyeweerd, *Twilight*, p. 6.

[55] But why should it? Gödel showed that a mathematical axiomatic system cannot prove all the arithmetic expressions that logic shows to be true.

other of his ideas. We listed Friesen's points of difference between Dooyeweerd and Vollenhoven, and one was that Dooyeweerd distinguished the modalities in the order in which they appeared phenomenologically in temporal experience and Vollenhoven said that the order was one of increasing complexity. García's notion is that the order is one of historical scientific discovery.[56]

Sooner or later the discussion has to reach the possibility of theoretical talk about God. The general problem of theoretical talk has already been broached, in that Dooyeweerd used his own peculiar boundaries to the theoretical, which effectively changed its meaning and this had ruled wide areas out of the theoretical. Within this banned region is God. Now García wants to claim that this is nothing more than mere Calvinism. He says, "Contrary to the scholastic metaphysics of Augustine, Anselm, and Thomas Aquinas, the reformers taught that what can only be known of God is what He wants to reveal about Himself".[57] Augustine was not a scholastic, and in Anselm's day scholasticism was barely getting going, but beyond that, we have come to the question of how far Calvin differed from

---

The other problem, usually mentioned as more influential than Gödel, is Bertrand Russel's discovery of paradoxes in Frege's set theory [the set of all sets that are not members of themselves]. Both of these suggest that every such theory requires that it be considered within a meta-theory, which perhaps means that logic is greater and more encompassing than mathematics. Van Til's transcendental argument, incidentally, confronts a similar obstacle as he compares the explanatory power of all theories, but in terms of what theory and logic?

Here is a thought experiment: For some consistent axiomatic theory of arithmetic, A, Gödel's result shows that there is a true arithmetical expression that is not provable in the system. (Gödel is said to have thought it might be a Diophantine equation.) Let us add this expression to A as an axiom, creating system A2. The result is now provable trivially in A2, but Gödel's result shows that for A2 there is a true expression not provable in it. As the power of proof of A2 includes all of A and more, this means that the Gödel statement of A2 is also not provable in A. By induction we can show that there is an infinity of arithmetic truths not provable in A. But suppose we identified one of these statements. Could we assume its opposite, derive a contraction, and thus prove it logically, even though it could not be proved from the axioms?

[56] García, *Reply*, pp. 56, 57.
[57] García, *Reply*, p. 53.

the scholastics. I will leave it to García to debate the rising tide of neo-scholastics in the seminaries. My interest is in what García says that Calvin did accept. "Of His essence, He has particularly revealed that He is a Trinity, an essence with a real distinction of persons or hypostases." Compare this to what Roy Clouser, whom García will later quote as an authority, says is possible in Dooyeweerdianism.

> The laws and properties of quantity are characteristics of the created things in the universe, and so are themselves also created. This must be borne in mind, that, for the Jewish and Muslim doctrine that God is one, as much as for the Christian doctrine that God is one-in-three. In each case, quantity is something created and assumed by God, and not intrinsic to God as he was prior to creating.[58]

The explicit contradiction to the Calvin quote shows that the Dooyeweerdian problem of the limitations of what can be said is definitely not equal to what Calvin thought were the limitations of what could be known about God.

García goes on to state "It is likely this restriction of theoretical theological thought to the revealed nature of God that leads Frame to say that Dooyeweerd presupposes that God is the created temporal reality!" Actually, Frame's line of thought is simple. Dooyeweerd says we can only have theoretical knowledge of the temporal. Theoretical knowledge is made up of propositions. Dooyeweerd expresses propositions about God. Therefore Dooyeweerd must consider God within the temporal. This unites God with the creation and is pantheism. It is fairly straightforward provided we consider the words in their normal meanings.

Of course, it was not only Frame who saw matters going in this direction, though based on different statements by Dooyeweerd. In particular, there is the problem of interpreting Dooyeweerd's non-dualism and his opposition to the idea of substance, as he did not want to allow being outside of God. Friesen discusses this in several places and tries a half-dozen solutions. He concludes that Dooyeweerd was a panentheist, though not a pantheist.[59]

---

[58] Roy Clouser, "Religious Language: A New Look at an Old Problem", *Rationality in the Calvinian Tradition*, ed. Hendrick Hart, Johan Van Der Hoeven, and Nicholas Woltersorff (University Press in America, 1983) p.401.

[59] Friesen, *Neo-Calvinism*, pp. 298, 347.

García's next interpretation is of Frame's objection to the everything-is-time idea in connection to thoughts, numbers, or propositions. Frame thinks that these do not have the characteristics of time. García concludes from this that Frame thinks that they are uncreated, and that therefore Frame is a Platonist. In García's mind the temporal is equated to the created and the non-temporal with the non-created. (But why? The supratemporal is also created.) But for Frame, not all things that are encountered in time have the nature of time. He would, however, say that all these are known to God. God does not have to wait for people to experience them in order for God to become aware of them. Is that Platonism?

After this, García turns to the heart and answers a series of questions posed by Frame. These, again, mainly arise from confusions that Frame experiences from not having gotten straight the idea of supratemporality. This is another case of the pairing of religious and philosophical terms. The heart is the supratemporal self. And, again, a follower of Vollenhoven would have to answer Frame's questions differently. For our purposes, the interesting point is that García resorts to quoting a series of Biblical texts, as though these were propositions from which theological truths could be deduced. Dooyeweedians do not play by their own rules. Once again the nature of obvious theoretical statements, which for Dooyeweerd are not theoretical statements, comes up. Too bad that Dooyeweerd did not learn Wittgenstein's lesson: "Whereof we cannot speak, thereof we must be silent."[60]

But García goes on to a very interesting point. Following D. Strauss, he rejects Dooyeweerd's idea of the synthetic intuition that unites the modalities. He thinks it is a Kantianism that Dooyeweerd should have jettisoned.[61] There is much more to this in the theory, in that each modality arises from its supratemporal kernel which is unified with the other modal kernels, that there are anticipations to the modalities, and retrocipations from the modalities back to the supratemporal, and also analogies between these anticipations and retrocipations of the various modalities. So they all carry some unify-

---

[60] Kierkegaard, though, took this lesson to heart, which is the main reason people find him so hard to interpret. Wittgenstein, who in his youth was a great reader of Kierkegaard, perhaps learned it from him.

[61] García, *Reply*, pp. 60, 61.

ing potential. Friesen expounds this *ad nauseam* and it might be interesting to those who do not think that this is all just made up.

I pointed out that Frame's treatment of law was very simplistic. He did not distinguish the ways that the Reformational thought used law and it quickly became apparent that he made no distinctions in his own thought. As I also have mentioned, it has been a criticism of Van Til that he did not deal with law effectively. All these things may be related. García begins by distinguishing three meanings of the word of God in the Scriptures: the Bible itself, Christ, and the law-word that governs the universe. This is very strange, as there are many instances where the word of the Lord came to someone and only part or none of it was recorded, the uses of word as commandment, etc. Word as commandment can be further distinguished as the word that brings about a result, as in creation and word that expresses an obligation for others which might be disobeyed.

There is a certain ambiguity in his expression "the system of laws, norms, and decrees that govern the universe." Does "govern that the universe" modify the whole phase, as I think most likely, or only "decrees"? In the latter case, he would here be allowing for commandments. In the former case, "norms" might be taken in some modal law-structure sense. It is hard to tell.

He goes on to discuss the "Greek" interpretation of John 1:1 as a sort of Demiurge, then continues to Augustine. Perhaps he is alluding to Augustine's appropriation of Neoplatonist philosophy. But what García is leading up to is to accuse Frame of Platonism again; "consistent with his Platonistic tendencies, Frame asserts that the law of God is 'essentially divine,' meaning that it is uncreated. This equates to saying that the law of God is equated with God Himself."[62]

Frame, though, is not a Platonist. Here he is showing his Biblicism. This type of Biblicism is best explained by instancing the case of another Van Tillian. Greg Bahnsen, in *Presuppositional Apologetics Stated and Defended,* has a section critiquing Gordon Clark. Here he rejects systematizing Scripture or even seeking a non-metaphorical meaning.[63] This Biblicism resists going beyond the language of Scripture in search of precise meaning. Of course, were these people

---

[62] García, *Reply,* p. 63.

[63] Greg Bahnsen, *Presuppositional Apologetics Stated and Defended* (Powder Springs, Georgia: American Vision Press, 2020) p. 190.

to do this consistently they would have to give up a claim to be Reformed. There is an irony here, in that this aspect of Van Tillianism is probably the endpoint of its absorption of Reformational ideas against deducing theology from Scripture.

García addresses Frame's questions about law.

> Regarding modal laws and norms, Frame raises the following questions: Is it true that a study of logic, history, linguistics, sociology, economics, aesthetics, jurisprudence, ethics, or theology will produce norms beyond those found in the Scriptures? Is it sinful to disobey them?[64]

He then suggests "Frame expresses himself as if the production of such norms were something strange to human life, or as if he wanted to separate human legislative activity from any reference to laws issued by God."

What Frame is trying to get at is whether there is some coherent idea of law and norm besides the imposition of some modal scheme with its inherent structural order. There is a big methodological problem here, as Frame is getting his information from J. M. Spier's 1954 book, *An Introduction to Christian Philosophy*, when Frame asks, "What is the relation of law to God? Is the law something created, or is it essentially divine? The formula that law is the 'boundary between God and the cosmos' obscures matters here because one would like to know what side of the boundary the boundary is on!" This idea of law as boundary is (2) on Friesen's list of differences between Vollenhoven and Dooyeweerd. It was Vollenhoven who said that law was the boundary.

Secondly, what is the relation of the content of Reformational law to natural law and to Biblical law? William of Ockham said "Every natural law is contained explicitly or implied in the divine Scriptures."[65] Is it so strange to ask how Reformational thought stands on this? Reformational thought seems to derive norms from modalities that are the product of theoretical speculation. Spier, as Frame reads him, says that the violation of such norms is sin. The examples

---

[64] García, *Reply*, p. 65.

[65] Francis Oakley, *Natural Law, Laws of Nature, Natural Rights: Continuity and Discontinuity in the History of Ideas* (New York and London: Continuum, 2005) p. 79.

Frame uses are errors in logic, language usage, or aesthetics.[66] What Frame wants to know is whether Scripture is sufficient for our knowledge of right and wrong, or do we need speculative philosophy to adduce the existence of modal spheres, and then deduce the norms that such spheres imply for existence? The latter seems to be the implication or even the explicit teaching of the Reformational thinkers.

García, without acknowledging these Reformational thinkers, gives his own different answer that the violation of modal norms is sin just in case it is also a violation of natural law.[67]

The same problem carries over to the topic of the application of Scripture, in particular the idea of positivization. García notes that Frame has said that "given that a 'positivization' or 'application' is valid only for a particular set of circumstances and for a certain time or place, this view implies that Scripture as we have it is dated, that is, it was temporal and is obsolete." García claims that "Frame here confuses the ceremonial and judicial laws of the Old Testament with 'Scripture'".[68] But Frame is not talking about the Mosaic law. Once again he was drawing from Spier and the Reformation thinkers he was encountering. The idea is that Scripture, as commandments, only applies directly in the faith modality. Even there, they only apply to their time. Thus we find the Reformational thinkers wanting to set aside much of the pastoral instruction that is in the epistles as the positivisation for the ancient Roman empire.

If we step back and examine how the controversy and Frame's book itself came about, it was that the Reformational thinkers were actively campaigning and trying to block the formation of explicitly Christian schools, because these violate modality distinctions, by applying the faith norms to the analytic modality. We can see how the theory of positivization plays a role in this, as it restricts where Scripture can be directly applied. In saying that the "same problem carries over" I am referring to Frame's source for understanding this, which is once again Spier's books and the activities of the Canadians.

In one of his more tortured sections, García addressed the "Reli-

---

[66] Frame cites Spier, *Introduction to Christian Philosophy*, pp. 119-122, and *What is Calvinistic Philosophy?*, p. 76ff.

[67] García, *Reply*, p. 66.

[68] García, *Reply*, p. 67.

gious Motive and Faith". Frame quotes from Dooyeweerd's *Twilight*, the "...radical and central, biblical theme of creation, fall into sin and redemption by Jesus Christ as the incarnate Word of God, in communion of the Holy Spirit", but notes: "Dooyeweerd, however, points out that 'it should not be confounded with the ecclesiastical articles of faith...' – that is, when he talks about the 'basic motive creation, fall, and redemption,' he is not talking about the *doctrines* of creation, fall, and redemption. The doctrines of creation, etc., can be studied theoretically; the 'basic motive' may not be, for it is addressed only to the heart of man and not to theoretical thought."

That Frame is not alone in this interpretation can be seen in how Friesen explains it.

> The Christian Ground-Motive is that of creation, fall, and redemption in Christ. But don't all Christians believe this? Not in the theosophical way that Dooyeweerd explained these ideas. In his view, these events happen outside of historical, cosmic time. Dooyeweerd says that creation, fall and redemption all occur in a *central sense in the supratemporal root*.[69]

> The fall was of man as religious root, which is why the temporal world, which has no existence in itself, fell with man.[70]

Friesen points out that Vollenhoven teaches the opposite, in that for him the cosmos alone has being, and that God is beyond Being. For Dooyeweerd redemption is universal and already accomplished in the supratemporal where everything is redeemed. This redemption is the substitution of Christ as the supratemporal center.[71]

Once again, though, Frame tangles himself up in his own attempt to make sense of this without taking into account the metaphysical model. García can then occupy himself with irrelevant references to Calvin, with showing where Frame's statements are wrong and ignoring the radically un-Christian nature of Dooyeweerd's ideas.

This continues with García's discussion of Frame's Philosophy and Theology section. Yet again Frame employs an approach of first supposing what Dooyeweerd must mean if he is to make sense and

---

[69] Friesen, *Neo-Calvinism*, p. 409.

[70] Friesen, *Neo-Calvinism*, p. 412.

[71] Friesen, *Neo-Calvinism*, pp. 390-395.

then critiquing the representation that he himself has constructed. This always gets Frame into trouble.

There is little point in trying to identify and trace all of Frame's misunderstandings. But something should be said about the phenomenon. It can arise easily when people set out to critique a position that practices evasion and obscurity. I recently encountered an instructive example in the attempt by Thomists to critique Van Tillianism. Repeatedly they attacked what were projections onto Van Til and his followers of their own way of doing things.[72] As I pointed out, Van Til cannot escape blame for this, as he habitually resisted making himself clear.

Frame's other major mistake, of mixing ideas and sources from Dooyeweerd with the Vollenhoven/Stoker schools, is less easy to understand. My experience with the Stoker group is that one had only to mention Dooyeweerd to bring out the crosses and cloves of garlic. They certainly did not want to be thought Dooyeweerdians! But Frame did not have the benefit of Friesen and his lifetime of study of these philosophies to explain the differences.

García has four main areas of error. First, he pretends that Dooyeweerdianism equals Reformational Theology when the Vollenhoven and then the South African stream are just as old, and are the majority version. García constructs his arguments in this imaginary world where only his version exists, except for a few late-coming followers who deviated from it and should be ignored. His second is to try to portray a Biblical and Calvinistic, and even somewhat scholastic Dooyeweerd in the area of natural law, who never existed. Third, he interprets Frame through a theory about what Frame thinks that is conjured up by García just as Frame created his own theories about what Dooyeweerd must mean. His last and largest error is to decontextualize the debate. Frame's book was written in the context of a campaign by the Reformational thinkers against Reformed theology and Christian institutions.

---

[72] Tim Wilder, *Divided Knowledge: Van Til & Traditional Apologetics* (Rapid City: Via Moderna Books, 2023).

EVALUATION

We have considered some basic questions about John Frame's debate with the Reformational philosophies. Did Frame understand these viewpoints? In many ways, his understanding fell short. Yet, in some *essential* matters, he did get his criticisms right. The qualification as essential is not so much for his grasp of the essence of the metaphysical and epistemic models of these philosophies, but where they touch, and differ from, key points of the orthodox Christian view.

Why did the seminary theologians take so long to confront the Philosophies and, when they did, do it so badly? The answer has to consider the two phases of the response. There were decades during which ideas from the Philosophies were absorbed and incorporated into the background structure of apologetics. Here we have to think of Westminster Seminary and Van Til, primarily. There were earlier critics, such as J. Oliver Buswell. While he could see the Idealist influences in Van Til, he did not know about the Reformational philosophies. The second phase is that of the Canadian invasion. Very aggressive and ideologically saturated groups – that is to say, radicalized – began to spread their ideas in a combative way. The sociology of this is that they were copying the New Left. It was this phase that brought on the battles at Westminster and in organizations such as school associations. Similarly, from the Westminster establishment point of view, the Philosophies went from being a source of tools that could be used in building apologetics taught to naive ministry students, to a source of tools for uppity youth to attack the uncritical and complacent faculty, who, as seemed apparent, didn't know the score. The form assumed by the response from the faculty was along the lines which they were used to fighting liberalism, including neo-orthodoxy. That is, they wrote articles on Scriptural authority. It was the same approach, and to an extent the same people, who, as we noted earlier, later failed at combating liberalism in the Christian Reformed Church. For people who touted their thinking as presuppositional, they showed a remarkable inability to identify and engage the presuppositions in these real-world debates.

Next, there was the both/and mentality of those promoting the Philosophies. In Frame's address to them, he points out that they are teaching views that are clearly against the historical Protestant view of Scripture, and yet when he presents that view, the Reformational spokesmen claim to agree with him! I am reminded of an illustration used by Francis Schaeffer (he was quoting someone else) that compared a Neo-orthodox theologian to a shopkeeper who keeps his goods hidden under the counter. When a customer comes in and asks for something, the shopkeeper brings it out and says, "That is *just* what we are selling here." In that way, the Neo-orthodox tried to be liberal and orthodox at the same time, while infiltrating their ideas everywhere. The Canadian Reformational people acted the same way to spread their philosophy.

There is another part of the answer to why the Westminster faculty did not see the problems with Reformational thought until the end of Van Til's thirty-five-year dalliance with the view. How did they understand it? The examination, which follows, of Van Til's understanding and use of the Philosophies is the beginning of the answer to this. Another question is, why has Frame's fifty-year-old response to the Reformational Philosophies suddenly become current?

VAN TIL'S INTERPRETATION OF THE REFORMATIONAL PHILOSOPHIES

Cornelius Van Til comments on his use of the Reformational Philosophies in his class syllabus of 1954.

> Now modern thought in general in largely controlled by the basic principles of modern philosophy. To evaluate these basic principles from the point of view of Christianity is therefore of paramount importance. Much help has been received on this matter from the writings of D.H.Th. Vollenhoven, and Herman Dooyerveerd [sic], of the Free University of Amsterdam, and from G. H. Stoker of Potchefstrom, South Africa.[73]

> Professors D.H. Th. Vollenhoven and Herman Dooyeweerd of the Free University of Amsterdam have worked out a Christian system of

---

[73] Cornelius Van Til, *A Christian Theory of Knowledge* (Westminster Theological Seminary, Syllabus, 1954) p. ii.

philosophy. They stress the fact that man should by virtue of his creation by God stand self-consciously under the law of God. And then they point out that since the fall man seeks his reference point in the created universe rather than in the Creator of the universe. They speak of non-Christian systems of philosophy as being immanentistic in character, refusing as they do to recognize the dependence of human thought upon divine thought. They indicate that on the basis of immanentistic philosophies there has been a false problematics. Immanentistic systems have absolutized one or another aspect of the created universe and have therewith been forced to do injustice to other equally important or more important aspects of the created universe. So for instance the Pythagoreans contended that all things are numbers. By thus taking the idea of the numerability of created things, which is the lowest and therefore least informative aspect of reality as the whole of it, as the final principle of interpretation, they have done grave injustice to other and higher aspects of reality. But in thus arguing for the significance of higher dimensions of created reality they do so by insisting that no dimension of created reality is done justice to unless it is seen in the perspective of its being subject with all other dimensions to the law of God for all created reality. In other words, there is a non-Christian as well as a Christian dimensionalism. The former too wants to maintain the reality and significance of higher dimensions than numerability and spatiality etc. But only the latter are able to keep from reducing all dimensions to one stark identity, for only the latter keeps the intellect of man within its place. It requires the intellect of man to find the dimensions of created reality, without legislating for reality. On the other hand even the highest form of non-Christian dimensionalism still is rationalistic in that it would reduce all reality, in all of its dimensions, to a penetrable system.

It is to be regretted that no full use of this well-worked out system of Christian philosophy can be made. It would carry us too far afield. But it will be greatly helpful to us in the analysis of the history of non-Christian philosophy.[74]

As this material dates from 1954, he had by then been associated with the Reformational Philosophies for nearly twenty years. His remarks show, in broad strokes, what his degree of understanding was.

Notable elements of what Van Til says here are:

1. He sees a single philosophy, jointly developed by Vollenhoven and Dooyeweerd.

---

[74] Van Til, *Knowledge*, pp. 32, 33.

2. Here, and elsewhere, he mentions Vollenhoven first, which may indicate that he relied primarily on Vollenhoven for his interpretation of the philosophy. This is in contrast to the mention of Dooyeweerd almost entirely in connection with the controversies at Westminster.
3. Van Til's interpretation of the role of law in the Reformational Philosophies is that man a) by virtue of his creation, b) should self-consciously, c) be under law. Van Til makes no effort to relate this to a particular context in the Reformational philosophies, that is to a) the modal law-structures, b) the juridic modality, or c) the positivization of Scripture in the faith modality. The rest of what Van Til has to say refers to the function and importance of the modal spheres, so he is most plausibly understood as referring to the law-structures. He does not recognize that for Dooyeweerd the creation, fall, and redemption Ground-motive is all supratemporal. Van Til is thinking of Adam in Eden in a historical sense. To be self-consciously under the law means to build your theory with the law-spheres and their modal sphere sovereignty limitations in mind, but Van Til does not distinguish this from temporal history.
4. Since the fall man seeks his "reference point" in the created universe rather than the Creator. Interestingly, Van Til picks up "reference point", a favorite term of his, but which Frame denigrates in his essay as one of the Philosophies' undefined metaphors (his Section 5). But (as Frame recognizes in his essay), in Dooyeweerd, this reference point is the supratemporal self, in the created heaven, not the Creator.
5. Non-Christian philosophy is immanentistic, refusing to recognize the dependence of human thought on divine thought. In Dooyeweerd's eternal/supratemporal/temporal scheme, the eternal is transcendent to the supratemporal, and the supratemporal is transcendent to the temporal. Conversely, the temporal (cosmic) is immanent in comparison with the supratemporal, and similarly the supratemporal is immanent compared to the eternal. The image of God refers to this hierarchy of expression, as God creatively expresses himself into the supratemporal, and man as God's image expresses himself into the temporal. Man, with his supratemporal heart, is a transcendent being. The immanence philosophies are those that start with the temporal and

Evaluation

try to explain experience solely in temporal terms. This has two problems. The first is that the temporal is fragmented into modalities, only one of which is the logical (theoretical), and building out of any one of these results in antinomies in the theory because of the fragmentation. The second problem is that such an immanence philosophy leaves out the supratemporal, which is where experience actually starts, so the philosophy is radically incomplete. This theory-making that is only in the immanent temporal is called by Dooyeweerd autonomous thought, as it is autonomous (disconnected) from the supratemporal. Of course, Vollenhoven would have a very different story.

6. Immanentistic philosophies create a false problematics. That is the antinomies mentioned in (5) because of the integrating explanatory role of the theory being in a particular modality of the fragmented temporal experience. Van Til, though, thinks of this as an "injustice" done to the parts of creation that do not get this priority. He sees this as not respecting the hierarchy in nature. There is an aspect to this in the Reformational philosophies, in that they hold that the modalities have a certain order, although it is explained differently by Dooyeweerd and Vollenhoven (and yet again by García). There is a striking analog to Thomism, in that the forms or archetypes are applied in a certain order to create the resulting species. The difference is that Thomism holds that the forms constitute God, whereas for the Philosophies the modes are strictly in creation. Van Til speaks of the "law of God for all created reality", but these law-structures all have their kernel in the supratemporal, where they are a unity and, in some sense, they are put there or determined by God, but it is man who expresses them into the cosmos.

7. Only Christian thought manages to avoid reducing all dimensions to "one stark reality". This seems to be Van Til explaining in his own way what he thinks are the implications of immanentistic thought. If it uses a modality as a starting point, it would reduce everything to that "one stark" modality, as he suggests with his example of Pythagoreanism. What the Reformational philosophies point to as the effect is antinomies. Actually, Dooyeweerd holds that these modalities began in a supratemporal unity (whether "stark" or not) and they only subsequently diverge into the richness of temporal experience. The problem,

then, is one for theoretical thought, where theoretical thought does not accept both the complexity and limitations of the situation under which it operates. Van Til's interpretation of "reduction" resulting from immanent philosophy is a move that he was used to from his Idealism, where the transcendent Absolute was needed for universals.

8. Van Til then describes the result to be avoided as "legislating for reality". This is a Van Tillianism, also adopted by Greg Bahnsen and K. Scott Oliphint. For Van Til it means using logic to determine what is possible. Typically he means using human reason to make deductions about God but, in this case, he seems to have in mind working from premises from a single modality-based theory.

9. Next Van Til explains this "legislating for reality" as a "rationalistic" reduction of all reality, in all its dimensions, to a penetrable system. This is a typical Van Til move. What would be similar in Dooyeweerd, is that a) the supratemporal is beyond theoretical analysis, because the theoretical is one modality in the temporal, and thus the supratemporal is not "logically penetrable". Frame ridicules this limitation a good deal in his essay. Also, b) there are problems with integrating the modalities, in that the logical is only one of them, so Dooyeweerd has to appeal to a supratemporal intuition that synthesizes them, so, here again, he is beyond the "logically penetrable". But even if reason does not accomplish this, it is the human mind, or self, that does. Van Til's point here is simply a preference for non-rational solutions such as Dooyeweerd offers, unless we try to interpret Van Til in terms of some major misunderstanding of at least Dooyeweerd's theory, and a transposition into some Van Tillian concept.

10. Van Til then says how he will use the Reformational Philosophies in his apologetics. This amounts to employing the Ground-motive analysis in his interpretation of the history of thought. That is, he will look for the use of a modality as an explanatory principle in historical thinkers and show how this is a reductionism that invalidates the analysis. The problem with this method is that it is distorting, and even when it has some application it is oversimplifying. This method, however, has in a large way entered the sort of worldview apologetics that is influenced by Van Til and his students.

Evaluation

In order to characterize Van Til's apologetics, however, a certain amount of complexity has to be allowed. In Van Til's example of the Pythagoreans, a particular modality, the numeric, takes over as the explanatory principle of nature. Dooyeweerd, however, had a scheme of three historical apostate Ground-motives. These are the form/matter of the ancient world, the scholastic nature/grace Ground-motive, and the Enlightenment nature/freedom one. These are expressed in terms of the resulting antinomy, not the underlying modal error. There is room for greater complexity in how these are related in a particular thinker, or for that matter, in a cultural practice.

Dooyeweerd's is not the only attempt to interpret cultural history through a particular mentality that was dominant at a time and place. The problem is always to find some pattern in the way that people thought about things that is general enough and basic enough to really explain the culture or a community within the culture and yet is not exceeded by the exceptions. There will always be dissenting historians who prefer the stubborn facts that do not fit the pattern over the pattern. Pragmatically, there is also the matter of evidence. What we have from the ancient world is scant, and what we have from more recent times is so voluminous and diverse (and it is the exceptions and innovations that draw the attention of both contemporaries and researchers) that is it hard to generalize on it.

From the ancient world, especially the Greeks, we have a body of literature (epic poems and drama) that they themselves picked out as especially meaningful in expressing their understanding of their existence. The drama had its origin in community religious rituals, as did the epics we have from Mesopotamia. If we read it according to the Ground-motive analysis, we are predetermined to find a conflict of antinomies caused by simplistic root explanations, as that is what Reformational thought dictates must be there. Seen differently, Greek philosophy could be seen as the frustrated attempt to find basic root explanations that were not there in the culture, so that the philosophical failures were only too evident.

There is a tradition of intellectual history, in search of the cultural ideals of various eras, that is not based on finding the predetermined Ground-motives, and makes fascinating reading, always bearing in mind the impossibility of making these really universal explanations. One particular attempt, in the explanation of the development of natural and positive law, is Lloyd L. Weinreb's *Natural Law and Justice*.[75] Interestingly, he finds that these always fail because they have built-in contradictions.

Van Til's thought seems to have changed in other ways through his contact with Reformational thought. His view of logic changed between his dissertation and his 1954 syllabus.[76] Other influences are hard to evaluate as they involve terminology that might have come from either Kuyper or Dooyeweerd such as autonomy and antithesis.

Van Til's Break From Dooyeweerd

We have Frame's explanation of Van Til's distancing himself from the Reformational Philosophy. While this was already discussed in connection with Frame's Section 14 on apologetics, a few more comments should be helpful. "During the last several years," Frame says, "Van Til has become much more critical of the Amsterdam movement." This places the break some fifteen years after the material quoted above to show how Van Til understood the philosophies during the period when he endorsed them. Perhaps "break" is too strong a term as well. Without getting lost in Frame's explanations we can consider two objections by Van Til, one complex and the other more simple.

The first concerns transcendental explanations and autonomous thought. Van Til had an apologetics based on the need for a transcendental explanation of the world (which he at first framed as experience). A transcendental explanation looks for what conditions or entities must exist for things to be the way they are. Van Til's arguments, generally, pointed to the Trinity. That is, he thought that the explanation has to be transcendent, creative, personal, and not purely simple. Dooyeweerd gave a place to transcendent explanations, but the furthest he would go was the need for an Origin beyond the supratemporal, i.e. in the eternal. For Van Til, that eliminated God in the important sense and thus amounted to autonomous thought because it was separate from God. Thus, for Van Til autonomous

---

[75] Lloyd L. Weinreb, *Natural Law and Justice* (Cambridge, Mass.: Harvard University Press, 1987).

[76] Tim Wilder, *Theosophy, Van Til, and Bahnsen*, section "Van Til and Logic", pp. 55, 56.

Evaluation 69

thought meant the lack of a beginning in a transcendental explanation (of the right sort).

For Dooyeweerd, autonomous thought is thought that leaves out its real origin. The origin of experience is in the supratemporal, coming out of the supratemporal self. The origin is not in the eternal, because man is not God. If Dooyeweerd were to start with the root of experience in man's eternal existence, that would be the same as positing a pantheistic explanation. To say that man's experience starts in God amounts to the same thing because it identifies it with divine experience. Thus Dooyeweerd does not define autonomous in terms of ultimate transcendent explanation, even though the supratemporal explanation concerns the self that transcends the temporal. Dooyeweerd's definition is about where and how human experience exists and functions.

Dooyeweerd's concept of autonomous thought does have more complexity to it than this. Theoretical thought creates a sort of artificial ego, needed for the temporal rational modality to regard the other modalities, which if taken for the actual independent self creates a dualism.[77] But here we only want to indicate that Dooyeweerd's philosophy is rich in such ideas. What is important is that Van Til did not seem to understand Dooyeweerd's idea of autonomy in the first place.

The second objection by Van Til is to the location of revelation by Dooyeweerd in the supratemporal, making it non-propositional. The implications of this are not so different from those of Van Til's own theory, as shown above, but the reasons are fundamentally different.

Of course, switch to Vollenhoven's thought and everything changes.

Why was the break so long in coming? Presumably, in the first few years of Van Til's teaching, at Princeton Seminary and at Westminster, he did not yet know about the Reformational Philosophies. Then, just before the end, he made his public criticisms.[78] For nearly the whole of his career, though, he was identified with this move-

---

[77] For Friesen's attempt to explain this, see his *Neo-Calvinism*, pp. 522, 523.

[78] To what extent was this difference pushed into the open by E. R. Geehan's, *Jerusalem and Athens* book project?

ment. His initial interest and inclination to agree with them is understandable in that he was a Kuyperian. Frame says, "Van Til was Kuyperian through and through, maintaining that the Bible 'speaks about everything' and encouraging his students and readers to apply the Scriptures of every sphere of life." He adds, "In the Kuyperian view, all the ills of society are essentially religious. They stem from people worshiping false gods. Either sinners worship the gods of some pagan ideology, or they give primacy to their own autonomous thought."[79] One could say that Van Til was even militantly Kuyperian. He and his fellow Dutch faculty at Westminster had an agenda. Their treatment of Gordon Clark, using Kuyperian theology, not the Confessions, as their standard for qualification for ministry showed that.

Van Til knew that Vollenhoven and Dooyeweerd were professors at the Free University that Kuyper had founded. He would have assumed that that was not possible unless a basic agreement between their views and the theological basis of the University and its parent denomination existed. But Vollenhoven and Dooyeweerd hid their views and their sources, as Friesen points out.[80] Dooyeweerd managed to stonewall the Curators of the Free University during their ten-year attempt to investigate him, which was never concluded. Still, Dooyeweerd thought he had been clear enough and he was puzzled that his "followers" clearly rejected his key ideas.[81]

For someone who was philosophically trained, as Van Til was, to miss the outline of Dooyeweerd's philosophy seems more than strange. Certainly, there were points that would have appealed to him. A number of similarities in the consequences and applications of their philosophies are pointed out in the foregoing discussion. Also, Van Til thought he had been gifted by them with a method to deal with the history of philosophical and theological thought. But to miss what they were saying for thirty-five years! One thing that gives this plausibility is that Van Til was equally blind to the disastrous implications of his own ideas.

But then, why did Westminster Seminary go along with it, and

---

[79] Frame, *Escondido Theology*, pp. 323, 324.
[80] Friesen, *Neo-Calvinism*, pp. 2, 21.
[81] Friesen, *Neo-Calvinism*, p. 23.

even make his ideas an unchallengeable core to their program? Why did the Orthodox Presbyterian Church go along with it? Why were the outside critics so ineffective? In one way the case of the critics can be explained in that they were mainly concerned with how Van Til differed from their own training and method and did not grasp the deep motivating elements in Van Til's perspective. Beyond a certain intellectual and institutional distance people simply did not respond to him. One notable exception was D. Z. Phillips, but writing long after Van Til's retirement. Phillips couldn't believe that Van Til actually meant what he said and tried to reply to what he thought Van Til meant.[82] The observation that presuppositionalists are really bad at spotting presuppositions, particularly their own, remains a major part of the explanation.

Today the Van Tillians are still trying to cover for him. None of them are willing to admit and examine the full scope of Van Til's involvement with the Reformational philosophies while recognizing what they really are. John Frame came the closest to pulling back the curtain. He at least took on the Philosophies, as he understood them, and he did admit that Van Til had endorsed them for years.

Who Was the Problem in 1972?

In the Preface, the fact that a practical problem initiated this debate was acknowledged and this raises the question, Was only one of the Reformational philosophies the cause of the troubles, and which one was it? In the case of the "battles" at Westminster Seminary, it seems clearly to have included the followers of Dooyeweerd in conflict with those who saw his thought as heretical. Even Friesen mentions this in his book.[83] Frame also mentions students who went away to weekend conferences.

But it seems to be the situation in the school associations that was decisive in bringing about Frame's critical analysis. That is, there was an active campaign against explicitly Christian schools based on a Reformational philosophy that did not countenance such a category.

---

[82] D. Z. Phillips, *Faith After Foundationalism: Plantinga-Rorty-Lindbeck-Berger — Critiques and Alternatives* (Boulder, Colorado: Westview Press, 1988). He discusses Van Til in the section dealing mainly with Plantinga.

[83] Friesen, *Neo-Calvinism*, p. 386.

The people whom I encountered who were mounting campaigns against what others were trying to do came out of the Institute for Christian Studies in Toronto (ICS) and they vigorously rebutted any statement that they were Dooyeweerdian. They claimed to be following G. H. Stoker, more generally within the Vollenhoven tradition. They were cookie-cutter New Left types, except that they had picked up on Reformational thought instead of Marcuse.

One of the stunts this group pulled was to attend InterVarsity's Urbana missions conference, bringing a trailer with a small press or duplicating machine of some kind. The ICS people would attend a session, then rush back to the trailer to write an analysis and rebuttal from the Reformational point of view, then go out to distribute their word to the attendees. People thought they were weird. It shows, however, their combative approach at the time.

In a note added in 2007 to his collection of small articles, "Dooyeweerd and the Word of God", Frame says:

> In the early 1970s, I got involved in some theological battles with the disciples of the great Dutch Christian philosopher Herman Dooyeweerd. These disciples had founded the Institute for Christian Studies (ICS) in Toronto, Canada. They held conferences throughout North America and published books and papers. ... Other ICS-influenced zealots tried to influence other Christian organizations (schools, churches, seminaries) to follow their lead.[84]

It seems likely, then, that both types of Reformational philosophy were sources of the problems that Frame was engaging. He again confuses Dooyeweerd with the Vollenhoven/Stoker group.

The Canadians Again

This debate over John Frame and the Reformational philosophies is a revival of a fifty-year-old debate. The debate has a particular origin in the campaign being waged against traditional Reformed thought, and even against traditional Kuyperianism in those places where Dutch thought enjoyed some privilege and had a chance of entry. It has been brought back to life because Reformational thought is once again trying to gain influence. This time, as far as I can tell (and I have

---

[84] John M. Frame, "Dooyeweerd and the Word of God", https://framepoythress.org/dooyeweerd-and-the-word-of-god/

not met any of the people involved), the seed was Joseph Boot and his Ezra Institute and their undue fondness for theology in wooden shoes. Stage two is the Cántaro Institute with its focus on Latin America. Evidently, they are effective as they have generated a vigorous response. The Cántaro Institute, with its stress on Reformational Philosophy, has found an audience that values that particular element, and as well having caused alarm to others who do not. A problem ensued, however, in that, practically, what was available on the critical side was the old material by Frame.

The big difference now is the *other* Canadian, J. Glenn Friesen. There is no longer a need for someone like Frame to write about Dooyeweerd. Friesen has put in the lifetime of study necessary to do it. Friesen is pro-Dooyeweerd. He would like to see Dooyeweerd's thought accepted and appreciated. But Friesen thinks that it need no longer travel under a Reformed cloak. In fact, Friesen claims that Dooyeweerd himself turned in an ecumenical direction and regretted ever having identified his philosophy with Reformed theology. While Friesen argues that Dooyeweerd and Vollenhoven started out working undercover, hiding their sources, and even hiding from outsiders how much they differed from each other, there is no longer any point to any of that. This makes Friesen's studies honest and refreshing.

Over on the Vollenhoven side, the diversity within the movement would make any study comparable to Friesen's very difficult and in the end cumbersome to read. Friesen has provided the background to Vollenhoven's early writing. Friesen doesn't like Vollenhoven's ideas, though, which seem to him to be a turning away at almost every point from Dooyeweerd's wonderful ideas.

THE BIG PICTURE

All the people that we have been discussing have been Kuyperians in some way, though definitely not in the same way. I want to argue that this is significant. We can consider the influence in two ways, the narrow Neo-Calvinist ideas and a broader but basic influence on thinking. The narrow elements are the usual concepts associated with Neo-Calvinist models: antithesis, sphere-sovereignty, autonomy, and worldview. Also, a certain mystical side of Kuyper, friendly to the supratemporal idea, should be added.

The broad elements are the ones that mattered in the end or, we could say, to the big picture. These are the Kuyper covenant and Common Grace. The two are connected and, yet, disconnected. The Kuyper covenant is the common covenant, more frequently called the Common Grace covenant. With this, Kuyper guaranteed a place for culture in Christian thinking. This works by placing culture, including civil government and law, under its own covenant, separate from the Covenant of Grace and the various covenants in the Bible that are subordinate to the Covenant of Grace. Thus culture was protected from being swallowed up by redemption. Culture no longer has to try to justify having a legitimate role in Christian thought by finding a place within the redemption program. The effect of this has been to disconnect culture and redemption and make it a problem to find a proper way to apply Biblical content to the common cultural area, as almost all the content can potentially be claimed for the redemption side of God's programs.

Common Grace is, in theory, administered under the common covenant, but it is generally thought of independently. Kuyper's Common Grace doctrine is the duct tape of his theology. It patches, holds together, supports, and closes gaps whenever these appear in the theological structure. It has no rules of its own that it must follow but just adheres and connects wherever a fixup is needed. It is generally understood as a sort of pressure for good and against evil that keeps things from being as bad as they could be. But Kuyper realized that its role needed some sort of explanation. It makes a difference whether Common Grace is thought of in terms of its covenant, as Meredith Kline eventually did, or as some general factor in creation, as became the way in the Christian Reformed Church. There it eventually invaded the redemption area and in 1924 precipitated a denominational split.

Cory Gress, in his essay, gave too large a place to Reformational philosophies in the production of the problems in the Christian Reformed Church but Reformational thought was able to work in synergism with general ideas that prevailed there. One was Common Grace, which came to be used as a battering ram against the Authority of Scripture. After all, if someone is having a problem with what Scripture teaches, it is because that person is following something else. And support for that something else can always be found by making it an expression or effect of Common Grace.

Evaluation

The Reformational people, meanwhile, had an ideology for narrowing the application of Scripture to the faith area and getting rid of older norms as obsolete positivizations. Further, the ongoing work of the Holy Spirit was being revealed in science, particularly the social sciences, as those sciences investigated the modal spheres. To follow that science was to obey God through his law-structures.

Therefore there is a case for considering the debate not merely as the problem of Reformational philosophies, but as the problem of Kuyperianism.

At some point, Kuyperianism lost its appeal in the Dutch denominations. They have moved on to more trendy liberalism and wokeness. The conservative remnants that came out of them are attracted to the other, Kuyper covenant, side of the theology in its present form as the Radical Two-Kingdom theology. They have started to supplement their theology, not from Reformational Philosophy, but from Thomism.

Eventually, Kuyperianism destroys whatever the Reformed thought where it is adopted. It does this by disrupting the basic covenantal system that unifies the theology. In time some other basis will be sought to provide support for the theology. Reformational philosophies have functioned in that role, but today they seem to be losing to Thomism. In Mexico, perhaps because of the historical experience with Romanism, Thomism does not have the same appeal and this may explain why Reformational philosophies are an attractive option. This, though, is a temporary phase. It may take more than a century for the process to work though, but in the end, there will simply be a speculative system adapting to the spirit of the times to try to remain relevant.

CITATIONS AND FURTHER READING

It is neither practical nor beneficial to try to create a bibliography of works about the Reformational Philosophy. The list would be massive, largely in languages not well-known internationally, and unobtainable. Even when obtainable, they remain turgid and incomprehensible. The list below includes works that are relevant as largely referenced in this discussion or explaining further the viewpoints intrinsic to this discussion.

Dooyeweerd, Herman, *In the Twilight of Western Thought*. There are multiple editions. A hardback was published in 1960 by Presbyterian and Reformed, having been edited by Henry Van Til from "basic material" from a series of popular lectures from a tour of North America conducted by Dooyeweerd. It was published by Craig Press, in their Modern Thinkers series with an Introduction by Rousas Rushdoony. It is included in *The Collected Works of Herman Dooyeweerd*, Series B, Volume 4 (Grand Rapids: Paideia Press, 2012), and this version is also available online.

Frame, John M., *The Amsterdam Philosophy: A Preliminary Critique*. Several editions: Pilgrim Press, 1972, and Harmony Press, also dated to 1972, that binds Frame's work with an essay by Leonard J. Coppes. Online without page numbering, https://framepoythress.org/wp-content/uploads/2012/08/FrameJohnAmsterdamPhilosophy1972.pdf A Spanish translation, *Crítica a la Filosofía Reformacional*, trans. Doner Bartolón (Villahermosa, Tabasco: Reforma Press, no date, but probably 2022) in combination with Un reporte desde el decierto by Cory Gress.

Friesen, J. Glenn, *Two Paths of Reformational Philosophy: Early Writings of Vollenhoven and Dooyeweerd*, p. 145. Online. https://www.academia.edu/105254020/Two_Paths_of_Reformational_Philosophy_Early_Writings_of_Vollenhoven_and_Dooyeweerd_by

Friesen, J. Glenn, *Neo-Calvinism and Christian Theosophy: Franz von Baader, Abraham Kuyper, Herman Dooyeweerd* (Calgary: Aevum Books, 215, 216, 2021)

Garciá de la Sienra, Adolfo, *Philosophy & Reformed Theology* (Jordan Station, Ontario: Cántaro Publications, 2024).

Gress, Cory, "A report from the desert". See above. Evidently it appeared first in English somewhere.

Spier, J. M., *An Introduction to Christian Philosophy* (Philadelphia: Presbyterian and Reformed, 1954).

Various essays by Van Til, Dooyeweerd, and R. D. Knudsen in E. R. Geehan, ed. *Jerusalem and Athens* (Phillipsburg, New Jersey: Presbyterian and Reformed, 1971).

Wilder, Tim, *Divided Knowledge: Van Til & Traditional Apologetics* (Rapid City: Via Moderna Books, 2023). An analysis of the Thomist critique of Van Tillian presuppositionalism showing how the critique is trapped by Thomist assumptions about science and logic and fails to take into account the Idealist and Reformational sources of Van Til's thought and their metaphysics molded his apologetics.

Wilder, Tim, *Theosophy, Van Til, and Bahnsen: How Neo-Calvinisn Deformed Apologetics* (Rapid City: Via Moderna Books, 2023). An account of how Idealism and half-digested Reformational philosophy, later supplemented by analytical ideas, left the Van Til tradition with an incoherent and implausible theory of knowledge.

INDEX

A
AACS 35, 39
Absolute in Idealism 24
Ames, William 36
Anselm 15, 53
Aquinas, Thomas 20, 36, 53
Augustine 53
Autonomous thought 15, 21, 23, 31–32
Averroes 37

B
Baader, Franz Xaver von 10, 30
Bahnsen, Greg 56, 66
Barth, Karl 37, 50
Being 10, 13, 20, 30
Biblicism 36, 57
Boehm, Jacob 9
Boot, Joseph 73
Buswell, J. Oliver 61

C
Calvin College 3–4, 6
Calvin, John 54
Canadian Reformed Churches 40–41
Cántaro Institute 1, 5, 73
Christian Marxism 46
Christian Reconstruction 2, 18
Christian Reformed Church 42, 61, 74
Christian schools 1, 28, 44
Church dogmatics 27
Clark, Gordon 24, 50, 56, 70
Clouser, Roy 18, 54
Common Grace 41, 74
Common sense 11–12
Coppes, Leonard J. 5
Creationist science 28

D
De Graff, Arnold 31
Demiurge 56
Dennison, William 46
Dooyeweerd, Herman
    fall, view of 16, 29
    In the Twilight of Western Thought 2, 6, 12, 18, 20, 26, 45
    law, view of 25, 56–57
    New Critique of Theoretical Thought 18

E
Ellul, Jacques 37
Erigena, John Scotus 20
Eternal 9–10, 14, 19–22, 30–31
Ezra Institute 73

F
Federal Vision 3
Fesko, J. V. 4
Frame, John

persons, view of 30–31
view of law 56
Free University of Amsterdam 6, 25, 39, 62, 70
Frege, Gottlob 53
Friesen, J. Glenn 5, 8, 10, 16, 18, 20, 25, 28–29, 33, 51, 54, 57, 59, 71, 73

G

García de la Sienra, Adolfo 5, 49
Gnosticism 20
Gödel, Kurt 52–53
Godfrey, Robert W. 44–45
Gress. Cory 5, 41, 74
Groen van Prinsterer, Guillaume 51
Ground-motives 3, 21, 39, 50
   creation, fall, redemption 12, 26, 32, 34, 51, 59
   Van Til's use of 21–22, 66–67

H

Human origins 42

I

Ideas/concepts distinction 14, 16
Individuality structures 9, 13, 30
Institute for Christian Studies 3, 72

J

Janse, Antheunis 10
Jordan, James 2

K

Kant, Immanuel 13, 16, 28, 55

Kantian idealism 9
Kingdom of God 29
Kline, Meredith G. 3, 29, 45, 74
Knudsen, Robert D. 6
Kuyper, Abraham 2, 10–11, 44, 46, 51, 68, 70, 73–75
   view of spirituality 12

L

Lewis, C. S. 43
Logicism 52

M

Mart, Hendrik 31
McConnel, Timothy L. 6
Meaning 16, 23–24, 28
Metaphysics 8, 10, 19, 27, 36, 39
Modalities
   different views of 10–11, 13
   law structures of 9, 13, 17, 19, 25, 29–30
   modes 17
   Nuclear moment of 9, 11, 13–14, 19
   sphere sovereignty of 9, 11
   time, in relation to 19, 52

N

Naïve experience 9, 11–13, 17, 19
Nash, Ronald 50
Natural law 57
Neo-Calvinism 9, 73
Neo-orthodoxy 33, 51, 62
New Age 43
New Left 61, 72
North, Gary 18

Index

O

O'Donnell, Laurence R. 7
Oakley, Francis 36
Ockham, William of 57
Oliphint, K. Scott 3, 41, 66
Olthuis, James 24, 39, 46
Orthodox Presbyterian Church 25, 71

P

Phenomenology 9
Phillips, D. Z. 71
Philosophia Reformata 6
Philosophical prolegomena 50
Philosophy of mind 19
Platonism 55–56
Plotinus 20
Positivisation 58
Positivization of faith-norms 26–27, 35, 64, 75
Postmillennialism 44
Pre-theoretical experience 11
Presupposition 14–15
Princeton Seminary 2, 4, 69
Propositions 13–14, 25, 45
Protestant Reformed Church 41

R

Radical Two-Kingdom theology 29, 44, 75
Real world 13
Reference of terms 16
Reformational philosophies
    failure to distinguish 12, 14, 25, 49, 60
    implications vs applications 29
    names of 6, 25, 49
    norms and sin in 29–30, 45, 58
    priority of 28
    Scriptural character of 11, 26–27, 60
Reformed Church in America 41
Reid, Thomas 11, 42
Revelation 22
    as expression to lower level 10, 12, 34
    different view of 7, 12, 25, 33–34
    openbaar 12
Runner, H. Evan 6
Rushdoony, Rusas J. 2, 18
Russel, Bertrand 53

S

Schaeffer, Francis 3, 62
Scholasticism 4, 7, 22, 28, 35, 39, 53
Science, theory of 52
Scrotenboer, Paul G. 39
Shepherd, Norman 7, 43–44
Spier, J. M. 21, 25, 29, 58
    An Introduction to Christian Philosophy 2, 12, 57
Steen, Peter J. 22, 39
Stellingwerff, Johan 20
Stoker, H. G. 6, 60
Strauss, D. 55
Suárez, Francisco 50
Supratemporal 29
    as created heaven 9
    as religious 14, 20
Supratemporal heart 10, 12, 19–20, 26–27, 55
Synods 50
Synthetic intuition 14–16,

28, 66

T

Temporal experience 9, 13–16, 22
Theoretical thought 9, 13–14, 16–17, 53–54, 66
Theosophy 9
Thomism 18, 47, 65, 75. See Also Aquinas, Thomas
Transcendence/immanence distinction 22, 64
Transcendental reasoning 31, 38, 68
Trinity 31, 54

U

Urbana missions conference 72

V

Van Til, Cornelius
   analogical knowledge 16, 23–24
   endorsement of Reformational Philosophy 2, 6, 8, 62, 70
   Idealism 24, 28
Van Til, Henry 18
Van Till, Howard J. 43
Verbrugge, Magnus 17–18, 25

W

Weinreb, Lloyd L. 68
Westminster. California 3–4, 44–45
Westminster Confession 23
Westminster Seminary 2–4, 6, 41, 45, 61–62, 69–70
   disputes at 7, 71
Wolterstorff, Nicholas 41, 46

Women elders 42

Y

Yale University 42

Z

Zylstra, Bernard 35–38

www.ingramcontent.com/pod-product-compliance
Lightning Source LLC
Chambersburg PA
CBHW031414040426
42444CB00005B/565